Managing Intense Anxiety Workbook

A TOOLBOX of REPRODUCIBLE ASSESSMENTS and ACTIVITIES for Facilitators

Ester R.A. Leutenberg
and John J. Liptak, EdD

publisher of therapy, counseling, and self-help resources

Duluth, Minnesota

Managing Intense Anxiety Workbook

publisher of therapy, counseling, and self-help resources

101 West 2nd Street, Suite 203
Duluth, MN 55802

800-247-6789

books@WholePerson.com
WholePerson.com

Managing Intense Anxiety Workbook
A Toolbox of Reproducible Assessments and Activities
for Facilitators.

Copyright ©2016 by Ester R.A. Leutenberg and John J. Liptak. All rights reserved. The activities, assessment tools, and handouts in this book are reproducible by the purchaser for educational or therapeutic purposes. No other part of this book may be reproduced or transmitted in any form by any means, electronic or mechanical without permission in writing from the publisher.

All efforts have been made to ensure accuracy of the information contained in this book as of the date published.

The author(s) and the publisher expressly disclaim responsibility for any adverse effects arising from the use or application of the information contained herein.

Printed in the United States of America

10 9 8 7 6 5 4 3 2 1

Editorial Director: Carlene Sippola
Art Director: Mathew Pawlak

Library of Congress Control Number: 2016937566
ISBN: 978-157025-345-4

Introduction

Using the *Managing Intense Anxiety Workbook*

Anxiety has been defined as a state of intense apprehension, uncertainty, and fear resulting mainly from the anticipation of a threatening event or situation, often to a degree that disrupts normal, everyday physical and psychological functioning. Fear is an emotional response to a <u>real or perceived threat</u>. Anxiety is anticipation of a <u>future threat</u>.

Anxiety is normal in the everyday life of all people. In fact, it can be a good thing. Anxiety motivates one to accomplish goals and warns a person of a dangerous situation. However, intense anxiety can involve debilitating symptoms. Some people persistently experience intense and excessive amounts of worry and fear about everyday situations. Sustained anxiety can lead to depression. This persistent anxiety and fear can interfere with daily activities. Often, these symptoms are difficult to control.

How Does Anxiety Manifest Itself?

Anxiety affects one's general well-being and manifests itself physiologically, behaviorally, and psychologically. Following are some of the ways that anxiety can affect participants:

- Anticipating the worst outcome
- Can't sit or stand still
- Chills
- Cold or sweaty hands and/or feet
- Difficulty concentrating
- Dizziness
- Dry mouth
- Feeling as if one's mind has gone blank
- Feeling powerless
- Feeling tense and jittery
- Feelings of apprehension
- Feelings of extreme panic, fear, and tension
- Heart palpitations
- Inability to act
- Inability to express oneself
- Inability to sleep and/or remain asleep
- Inexplicable feelings of dread
- Irritability
- Muscle tension
- Nausea
- Over-alertness for signs of danger
- Racing mind
- Shortness of breath
- Tingling of hands and/or feet

Our goal for this workbook is NOT to diagnose a mental illness, or even for the facilitator to make that diagnosis from this workbook's content. Our goal is to touch on some of the symptoms and possibilities, create realizations, and provide coping methods which will help people to go forward and perhaps consider the possibility of the need for medications and therapy.

Our other goal is to help participants recognize that other people have the same issues. No shame should be connected to them, nor should mental health issues of any kind be stigmatized.

In this workbook, we are using the phrase *mental health issues* to include all types of anxiety issues, from having a few anxiety problems to a serious, extremely intense anxiety issue.

Managing Intense Anxiety Workbook

"Normal" Anxiety vs. Intense Anxiety Disturbances

Anxiety is an inevitable part of everyday life for most people. Some anxiety is actually an appropriate emotional response to a variety of situations that people encounter. The assessments and activities in this workbook can be valuable tools for helping participants deal effectively with "normal" everyday anxiety that they experience, as well as more intense anxiety disturbances.

Anxiety manifests itself in the everyday life of most people in many different ways.

Some of the most common types of everyday, "normal" anxiety:
- **Situational Anxiety** – Feelings of apprehension and dread related to a specific situation such as starting a new job, moving to a new community, or learning about a new illness.
- **Anticipatory Anxiety** – Feelings of apprehension and dread when one confronts something that has been frightening in the past, or that has resulted in a negative experience such as speaking in front of a large group of people.

Anxiety Disturbances – These can be distinguished from the everyday, "normal" anxiety because they are more intense (panic attacks), last longer (often months or years instead of going away after an anxiety-producing situation), and interfere with a person's ability to function effectively in daily life (i.e., inability to function in a job).

Different types of disturbances related to thinking and behavior are conveyed and expressed in different forms:
- **Panic Disorder:** People have feelings of extreme terror that strike suddenly and often without any warning. People with panic disorder often experience sweating, chest pain, and/or heart palpitations. They feel as if they are out of control during one of their attacks of fear, and they attempt to avoid places where panic attacks have occurred in the past.
- **Social Anxiety Disorder:** People have feelings of overwhelming worry and experience extreme self-consciousness in everyday social situations. These worries include the fear that others will judge them harshly, they will do something that may be embarrassing, and the fear of being ridiculed by other people. People with this disorder often are very anxious being around people and have a difficult time talking to others. They will stay away from places where there are other people and have a hard time making and keeping friends.
- **Generalized Anxiety Disorder:** People exhibit excessive, extreme, and/or unrealistic worry and tension, even if there is nothing (or very little) to be worried and/or tense about. People with this disorder may be worried about just getting through the day and doing everyday tasks. They often have trouble falling and staying asleep, inability to relax, and trouble concentrating.
- **Specific Phobias:** People experience intense, unwarranted fears about an object or a situation. The fear involved in a phobia is usually inappropriate for the object or the situation and may cause people to avoid specific everyday situations in order to avoid the object or the situation. Some common phobias include snakes, speaking in public, clowns, fear of situations where escape from bad things is perceived as difficult. This represents an intense fear resulting from real or imagined exposure to a wide range of situations.
- **Substance-Induced Anxiety Disorder:** People experience anxiety caused by substance utilization or withdrawal.
- **Anxiety Disorder Due to Another Medical Condition:** People have anxiety attacks that can be directly attributed to an existing medical condition (often diagnosed with cancer), and it often parallels the course of the illness.
- **Obsessive-Compulsive Disorder:** People have recurring repetitive thoughts that will not dissipate (obsessions) and/or engage in ritual behaviors to dispel anxiety (compulsions).

Introduction

How the *Managing Intense Anxiety Workbook* Can Help

People who experience intense anxiety are likely to find it difficult to function in everyday life due to the symptoms associated with anxiety. The assessments and activities in this workbook are designed to provide facilitators with a wide variety of tools to use in helping people manage the intense anxiety in their lives more effectively. Many choices for self-exploration are provided for facilitators to determine which tools best suit the unique needs of their clients.

The purpose of this workbook is to provide a user-friendly guide to short-term assessments and activities to help people manage their anxiety, and the stress that often triggers it, and to give them a greater sense of well-being. In addition, this workbook is designed to help provide facilitators and participants with tools and information needed to overcome the stigma attached to intense anxiety issues.

In order to help participants cope successfully with stress and the subsequent anxiety, facilitators need to have a variety of assessments and activities to help their participants open up and begin to feel as if they can manage their anxiety to begin living a more calm and peaceful life. The *Managing Intense Anxiety Workbook* provides assessments and self-guided activities to help participants understand the intensity of their issues and how they can lead a more effective life.

When to Worry?

Symptoms related to intense anxiety can be very complex and difficult to cope with. The good news is that people can develop the skills needed to manage the symptoms and progress forward to begin enjoying life more. Undergoing the stress that accompanies many of the mental health issues can be a very frightening way to live. **People who experience intense anxiety and stress over time are at risk of developing a serious mental or physical illness and need to seek a medical professional.**

Suicide Warning!

People who experience intense anxiety may feel suicidal, have suicidal thoughts, and make plans for committing suicide. Sometimes they think that the only way to escape the physical, psychological, and emotional pain is to attempt suicide. Remember to take any talk about suicide or suicidal acts very seriously.

Signs of Suicidal Thoughts

- Calling or visiting people to say goodbye
- Engaging in reckless actions
- Expressing feeling of being trapped with no way out
- Expressing severe hopelessness about the future
- Giving away possessions
- Increasing use of harmful substances
- Talking about killing or harming oneself
- Making a plan for dying by suicide
- Purchasing a weapon
- Putting legal affairs in order
- Withdrawing from family, friends, and activities of interest in the past

Serious Mental Illness

If participants have a serious mental illness, they need to do much more than complete the assessments, activities and exercises contained in this workbook. They need to be taken seriously and facilitators can take an active role in their finding help immediately. All disturbances related to intense anxiety need to be thoroughly evaluated by a medical professional, and then treated with an appropriate combination of medication, and group and/or individual therapy.

Format of the *Managing Intense Anxiety Workbook*

The *Managing Intense Anxiety Workbook* is designed to be used either independently or as part of an established mental health issue program. You may administer any of the assessments and the guided self-exploration activities to an individual or a group with whom you are working, and you may administer any of the assessments and activities over one or more days. Feel free to pick and choose those that best fit the outcomes you desire. The purpose of this workbook is to provide facilitators who work with individuals and groups who may be experiencing intense anxiety issues with a series of reproducible activities that can be used to supplement their work with participants. Because these activity pages are reproducible, they can be photocopied as is, or you may adapt them by whiting out and writing in your own changes to suit the needs of each group, using that page as your master-copy to be photocopied for each participant.

Assessments

Assessments establish a behavioral baseline from which facilitators and participants can gauge progress toward identified goals. This workbook will supplement the facilitator's work by providing assessments designed to measure client change in those behavioral baselines. In order to do so, assessments with scoring directions and interpretative materials begin each module. The authors recommend that you begin presenting each topic by asking participants to complete the assessment. Facilitators can choose one or more or all of the activities relevant to their participants' specific needs and concerns.

Each of the awareness modules contained in this workbook begin with an assessment for these purposes:
- To assist participants to feel a part of the treatment-planning process.
- To help facilitators gather valuable information about their participants.
- To help facilitators identify patterns that are negatively affecting a participant.
- To help facilitators in the measurement of change over time.
- To help facilitators to develop a numerical baseline of behavior, attitude, and personality characteristics before they begin their plan of treatment.
- To prompt insight and behavioral changes in participant's lives.
- To provide participants with a starting point to begin to learn more about themselves and their strengths and limitations.
- To use as pre-tests and post-tests to measure changes in behavior, attitude, and personality.

Assessments are a great aid in developing plans for effective change. Be aware of the following when administering, scoring, and interpreting the assessments in this workbook:
- The purpose of these assessments is not to pigeonhole people, but to allow them to explore various elements of themselves and their situations.
- This workbook contains self-assessments and not tests. Traditional tests measure knowledge or right or wrong responses. For the assessments provided in this workbook, remind participants that there are no right or wrong answers. These assessments ask only for opinions or attitudes.
- The assessments in this workbook have face value, but have not been formally normed for validity and reliability.
- The assessments in this workbook are based on self-reported data. In other words, the accuracy and usefulness of the information is dependent on the information that participants honestly provide about themselves. Assure them that they do not need to share their information with anyone. They can be honest!
- Remind participants that the assessments are exploratory exercises and not a judgment of who they are as human beings.
- The assessments are not a substitute for professional assistance. If you feel any of your participants need more assistance than you can provide, refer them to an appropriate medical professional.

(Continued on the next page)

Introduction

Format of the *Managing Intense Anxiety Workbook* (Continued)

Assessment Script

When administering the assessments contained in this workbook, please remember that the assessments can be administered, scored, and interpreted by the client. If working in a group, facilitators should circulate among participants as they complete assessments to ensure that there are no questions. If working with an individual client, facilitators can use the instruction collaboratively.

Please note that as your participants begin the assessments in this workbook, the participants' instructions italicized below are meant to be a guide, so please do not feel you must say them word for word.

Tell your participants: *You will be completing a quick assessment related to the topics we are discussing. Please remember that assessments are powerful tools if you are honest with yourself. Take your time and be truthful in your responses so that the results are an honest reflection of you. Your level of commitment in completing the assessments honestly will determine how much you learn about yourself.*

Allow participants to turn to the first page of their assessment and read the instructions silently to themselves. Then tell them: *All of the assessments have similar formats, but they have different scales, responses, scoring instructions, and methods for interpretation. If you do not understand how to complete the assessment, ask me before you turn the page to begin.*

Then tell them: *Before completing each assessment, be sure to read the instructions. Because there is no time limit for completing the assessments, take your time and work at your own pace. Do not answer the assessments as you think others would like you to answer them or how you think others see you. These assessments are for you to reflect on your life and explore some of the barriers that are keeping you from living a more satisfying life.*

Make sure that nobody has a question, then tell them: *Learning about yourself can be a positive and motivating experience. Don't stress about taking the assessments or discovering your results. Just respond honestly and learn as much about yourself as you can.*

Tell participants to turn the page and begin answering with Question 1. Allow sufficient time for all participants to complete the assessment. Answer any questions. As people begin to finish, read through the instructions for scoring the assessment. Have participants begin to score their assessment and transfer their scores for interpretation. Ask if anyone has questions about how to do the scoring.

Review the purpose of the interpretation table included after each assessment. Tell the participants: *Remember, this assessment was not designed to label you. Rather, it was designed to develop a baseline of your behaviors. Regardless of how you score on an assessment, consider it a starting point upon which you can develop healthier habits. Take your time, reflect on your results, and note how they compare to what you already know about yourself.*

After participants have completed, scored, and interpreted their assessment, facilitators can use the self-exploration activities included in each module to supplement their traditional tools and techniques to help participants function more effectively.

(Continued on the next page)

Format of the *Managing Intense Anxiety Workbook* (Continued)

Self-Exploration Activities

This workbook will provide self-exploration activities that can be used to reduce stress and decrease anxiety. These activities, included after each of the assessments, will prompt self-reflection and promote self-understanding. They use a variety of formats to accommodate all learning styles, foster introspection, and promote pro-social behaviors, life skills, and coping skills. The activities in each module correlate to the assessments to enable you to identify and select activities quickly and easily.

Self-exploration activities assist participants in self-reflecting, enhancing self-knowledge, identifying potential ineffective behaviors, and teaching more effective ways of coping with anxiety. They are designed to help participants make a series of discoveries that lead to increased social and emotional competencies, as well as to serve as an energizing way to help participants grow personally and professionally. These brief, easy-to-use self-reflection tools are designed to promote insight and self-growth.

Many different types of guided self-exploration activities are provided for you to pick and choose the activities that are most needed by your participants and the ones that will be most appealing to them. The unique features of the exploration activities make them user-friendly and appropriate for a variety of individual sessions and group sessions.

In some activities, participants will have the opportunity to engage in these ways:
- Explore how they could make changes in their lives to feel better. These activities are designed to help participants reflect on their current life situations, discover new ways of living more effectively, and implement changes in their lives to accommodate these changes.
- Journal as a way of enhancing their self-awareness. Through journaling prompts, participants will be able to write about the thoughts, attitudes, feelings, and behaviors that have contributed to, or are currently contributing to, their current life situation. Through journaling, participants are able to safely address their concerns, hopes, and dreams for the future.
- Explore their intense anxiety issues by examining their past for negative patterns and learning new ways of dealing with them more effectively in the future. These activities are designed to help participants reflect on their lives in ways that will allow them to develop healthier lifestyles.

Take-Away Skills

Take-Away Skills for each Module Following each Module Cover Page
Conditions and Behavior, Frequency and Duration, and/or Accomplishment statements for each activity may be used in educational and/or treatment planning. They may also be used to measure progress toward goals. These skills promote real life outcomes and behavioral changes.

Introduction

The Stigma Awareness Approach

It is important that facilitators keep an open mind about mental health issues and the stigma attached to people experiencing these issues. Rather than thinking of people as having a mental disorder, or being mentally ill, the ***Erasing the Stigma of Mental Health Issues through Awareness*** series is designed to help facilitators diminish the stigma that surrounds people suffering from intense anxiety issues. Stigmas occur when people are unduly labeled, which sets the stage for discrimination and humiliation. Facilitators are able to help to erase the stigma of mental illness through enhancing awareness of the factors that activate the issues, accentuating the depth of the issues, and accelerating awareness and understanding.

To assist you, a module titled ***Erasing the Stigma of Mental Health Issues*** is included to provide activities to help erase the stigma associated with intense anxiety issues.

The Awareness Modules

The reproducible awareness modules contained in this workbook will help you identify and select assessments and activities easily and quickly:

Module I: Signs of Stress Symptoms
   This module will help participants explore the signs of stress in their lives, recognize the symptoms of anxiety, and learn tools to begin to help decrease the anxiety.

Module II: Need for Control
   This module will help participants explore the various ways they need to be in control of their lives.

Module III: Social Approval
   This module will help participants explore the various ways that their need for the approval of others affects their functioning in social situations.

Module IV: Perfectionism
   This module will help participants explore ways that their need to be perfect and mistake-free, as well as their determination to achieve unrealistic standards can cause anxiety.

Module V: Erasing the Stigma of Mental Health Issues
   This module will help participants explore the stigma of having intense anxiety and the impact that the stigma has on them.

Our thanks to these professionals who make us look good!

Art Director	—	Mathew Pawlak
Editorial Director	—	Carlene Sippola
Editor and Lifelong Teacher	—	Eileen Regen, M.ED., CJE
Reviewer	—	Jay Leutenberg, CASA
Reviewer	—	Carol Butler, MS Ed, RN, C
Reviewer	—	Loretta Behrmann, BS Ed

Managing Intense Anxiety Workbook

Table of Contents

Module I – Signs of Stress Symptoms 15
Take Away Skills Emphasized in Each Activity Handout 16-17
The Signs of Stress Symptoms Introduction and Directions 19
The Signs of Stress Symptoms Scale 20-21
Scoring Directions 22
Profile Interpretation 22
Scale Descriptions 22
Stress in My Work Life 23
Stress Associated With My Relationships 24
My Stress Triggers 25
Thoughts about My Stress 26-28
Picturing My Stress – NOW and THEN 29
Worry-Work 30
Worry Self-Talk 31
Recognizing Intense Anxiety Situations 32
My Anxiety Symptoms 33
Anxiety Tension 34
Effects of Anxiety 35
You Have Been Asked … 36
Basic Anger Management Tools 37
My Coping Strategies 38
Quick Meditation 39
My Kryptonite 40

Introduction

Table of Contents

Module II – Need for Control 41
   Take Away Skills Emphasized in Each Activity Handout 42-43
   Need for Control Introduction and Directions 45
   Need for Control Scale 46
   Scoring Directions 47
   Profile Interpretation 47
   Scale Descriptions 47
   Control or Not? 48
   Changes in My Life 49
   My "IF" Fears 50
   Go to Your Fears 51
   Doodling 52
   Taking Action to Reduce Anxiety 53
   Over and Over and Over Again! 54
   Hocus-Focus 55
   What's the Worst Thing? 56
   From a Self-Fulfilling Prophecy to Imagining the Best 57
   Staying in the Present 58
   Deep Breathing 59
   Relaxing Your Body 60
   Mindfulness 61
   Mindfulness Journaling 62

Managing Intense Anxiety Workbook

Table of Contents

Module III – Social Approval 63
    Take Away Skills Emphasized in Each Activity Handout 64-65
    Social Approval Scale Introduction and Directions 67
    Social Approval Scale 68
    Scoring Direction 69
    Profile Interpretation 69
    Scale Descriptions 69
    Events When I Feel Anxious 70
    People with Whom I Feel Anxious 71
    Situations Where I Feel Anxious 72
    Ways I Avoid Social Situations 73
    Social Situations Realities 74
    Need for Approval 75
    Validation 76
    I'm Good Enough! 77
    Rejection, Abandonment, and Disapproval 78
    Challenge Negative Thinking 79
    Positive Self-Talk Scripts 80
    Meet New People 81
    Self-Appreciation 82
    Accepting Myself 83

Introduction

Table of Contents

Module IV – Perfectionism 85
   Take Away Skills Emphasized in Each Activity Handout 86-87
   Perfectionism Introduction and Directions 89
   Perfectionism Scale 90
   Scoring Directions 91
   Profile Interpretation 91
   Scale Descriptions 91
   Criticizing Myself 92
   Criticizing Others 93
   Handling Criticism from Others 94
   Perfectionistic Thinking 95
   How I Feel When I am Being a Perfectionist 96
   Perfectionistic Thoughts 97
   I Must be Perfect 98
   A Perfectionism Affermations 99
   A Perfectionistic Contract 100
   The Good and the Bad 101
   Underlying Perfectionistic Reasons 102
   Small Steps in Setting Realistic Goals 103
   My Perfectionistic Moments 104
   Respecting and Loving Myself 105
   The Positive Me 106

Managing Intense Anxiety Workbook

Table of Contents

Module V – Erasing the Stigma of Mental Health Issues 107
- Erasing the Stigma of Mental Health Issues Introduction...............108
- Two Types of Mental Health Stigma.....................................109
- The Stigma of Intense Anxiety – THE PAST.............................110
- The Stigma of Intense Anxiety – THE PRESENT.........................111
- Speak Your Mind 112
- If We Stamp Out the Stigma … 113
- Glenn Close said … 114
- Effects of Anxiety Issues 115
- The Stigma of Going to a Mental Health Therapist 116
- Will You Speak Out? 117
- My Negative Thoughts 118
- Focus on Your Strengths..119
- Ways I Try to Minimize My Anxiety Issues 120
- Ways I am Treated 121
- Self-Doubt...122
- A Poster about the STIGMA of People Who Experienced Anxiety 123
- A Poster about ACCEPTANCE of People Who Experienced Anxiety......124
- DE-STIGMA-TIZE with the Facts about Mental Health Issues............125
- Coping with the Stigma of an Intense Anxiety Issue 126
- Speak Out Against Stigmas...127

MODULE I

Signs of Stress Symtoms

Anxiety does not empty tomorrow of its sorrows, but only empties today of its strength.

~ Charles Spurgeon

Name _____

Date _____

Module I – Take-Away Skills

We have included skills for most of the handouts in each Module, *Conditions and Behavior* (1), *Frequency and Duration* (2), and/or *Accomplishment* (3) statements for each activity may be used in educational and/or treatment planning, and also used to measure progress toward goals. These Take-Away skills promote real life outcomes and behavioral changes. Feel free to add additional skills for each activity.

Examples

1. **Conditions and Behavior** – a skill or healthy habit to replace a previous less effective behavior/habit.
   - Now, I … *(less effective or undesired behavior)*
     when I … *(when do I do this?)*.
     Instead I will … *(more effective or desired new behavior)* in ___ out of ___ opportunities.
2. **Frequency and Duration** – a skill or healthy habit not necessarily tied to a condition or previous behavior.
   - I will *(describe the behavior)* _____ times per _____.
3. **Accomplishment** – an outcome that is a one-time accomplishment.
   - I will *(describe the accomplishment)* by _____ *(date)*.

Take-Away Skills Examples

Stress in My Work Life 23
   Conditions and Behavior
   - Now, I … *experience nausea*
     when … *something unexpected comes up at work.*
     Instead I will … *take a walk to clear my head 4 out of 4 opportunities.*
   - Now, I … *become upset*
     when … *I do not feel supported at work.*
     Instead I will … *talk to my supervisor about it 4 out of 4 opportunities.*

Stress Associated with Relationships 24
   Conditions and Behavior
   - Now, I … *say "yes"*
     when I … *am asked to do something I don't really want to do.*
     Instead I will … *definitively say no 4 out of 4 opportunities.*

Take-Away Skills Examples (Continued)

Thoughts about My Stress..26-28
   Conditions and Behavior
   - Now, I … *experience racing thoughts*
     when I … *lay down for bed.*
     Instead I will … *write my thoughts down in a journal 5 out of 5 opportunities.*

Picturing My Stress- NOW and THEN..29
   Accomplishment
   - I will … *draw a picture of what I want my stress to look like in order to gain control over it by tomorrow.*

Worry Self-Talk..31
   Conditions and Behavior
   - Now, I … *tell myself that I am a failure*
     when I … *have to speak in front of others.*
     Instead I will … *repeat a positive mantra to myself 4 out of 4 opportunities.*

Basic Anxiety Management Tools..37
   Frequency and Duration
   - I will … *go for a walk to reduce my anxiety 5 times a week during my lunch break, for a month.*
   - I will … *say the Serenity Prayer out loud to myself 1 time every morning for a month.*
   - I will … *exercise for 30 minutes, 3 times a week for a month.*
   - I will … *journal my eating habits 1 time a day for a week.*

   Conditions and Behavior
   - Now, I … *avoid going to the store*
     when I … *am by myself.*
     Instead I will … *use visualization to independently go to the store 4 out of 4 opportunities.*

Managing Intense Anxiety Workbook

Signs of Stress Symptoms Scale
Introduction and Directions

People who feel intense anxiety often experience a wide variety of physical, emotional, and psychological symptoms. A key factor in overcoming their anxiety is to develop the ability to identify signs of stress when they begin to present themselves, and to have knowledge of a few techniques for quickly calming the anxiety.

This scale contains two scales of twenty statements each, related to how well you recognize the signs of stress that lead to anxiety. Read each of the statements and decide how much the statement describes you.

- If the statement describes you a lot, circle the number under that column next to that item.
- If the statement describes you sometimes, circle the number under that column next to that item.
- If the statement describes you only a little, or not at all, circle the number under that column next to that item.

In the following example, the circled number under "A Lot" indicates the statement is very descriptive a lot of the time of the person completing the scale.

When I begin to feel stressed, I recognize that…	A Lot	Sometimes	Little/None
I am trembling and shaking	3	2	1

This is not a test. Since there are no right or wrong answers, do not spend too much time thinking about your answers. Be sure to respond to every statement.

(Turn to the next page and begin.)

Managing Intense Anxiety Workbook

Signs of Stress Symptoms Scale P

When I begin to feel stressed, I recognize that…	A Lot	Sometimes	Little/None
I am trembling and shaking	3	2	1
My heart is beating faster	3	2	1
I am experiencing intense worry/fear	3	2	1
I am lightheaded or dizzy	3	2	1
I can hardly breathe	3	2	1
I feel very cold	3	2	1
My chest feels tight	3	2	1
My hands are tingly	3	2	1
I have sweaty palms	3	2	1
I feel sick	3	2	1
My hands or feet feel numb	3	2	1
I have sleeping problems	3	2	1
I have headaches	3	2	1
I have muscle tension or aches	3	2	1
I have difficulty swallowing	3	2	1
I have stomach problems and/or nausea	3	2	1
I get dry skin and/or rashes	3	2	1
I use the restroom more often than usual	3	2	1
I become overly tired	3	2	1
I get hot flashes	3	2	1

Scale P = _____

Signs of Stress Symptoms Scale E

When I begin to feel stressed,	A Lot	Sometimes	Little/None
I cry easily and/or often	3	2	1
I cannot control my fears	3	2	1
I am very worried and cannot control it	3	2	1
I don't feel calm in certain situations when I need to	3	2	1
I have fears that may be foolish	3	2	1
I become short-tempered	3	2	1
I get angry easily	3	2	1
I am easily exhausted	3	2	1
I have difficulty concentrating	3	2	1
I feel sad for no reason at all	3	2	1
I am unable to relax	3	2	1
I have irrational thoughts	3	2	1
I avoid situations where I should be present	3	2	1
I avoid people with whom I need to be with	3	2	1
I avoid activities I used to enjoy	3	2	1
I become irritable very easily with others	3	2	1
I have unhappy flashbacks	3	2	1
I have terrible nightmares or bad dreams	3	2	1
I fear losing control	3	2	1
I see everything in a negative way	3	2	1

Scale E = _____

Go to the Scoring Directions

Managing Intense Anxiety Workbook

Signs of Stress Symptoms Scales P and E Scoring Directions

Your ability to recognize the signs of stress that lead to anxiety can help you to determine when anxiety is becoming a problem. This will allow you to take action to reduce the feelings of anxiety. This scale is designed to help you explore those signs of stress.

Add the numbers that you circled. Your totals will range from 20 to 60 on each scale. Then, transfer your totals to the spaces below:

Scale P - Physical Symptoms = _____

Scale E - Emotional Symptoms = _____

Profile Interpretation – Scale P - Physical Symptoms

Place an X on the line below, indicating the score of your physical anxiety symptoms:

20   30   40   50   60

SOME SYMPTOMS   MANY SYMPTOMS

Profile Interpretation – Scale E - Emotional Symptoms

Place an X on the line below, indicating the score of your emotional anxiety symptoms:

20   30   40   50   60

SOME SYMPTOMS   MANY SYMPTOMS

Scale Descriptions

Scale P - Physical Symptoms – People scoring High on this scale tend to experience many distressing physical symptoms when they are stressed and become very anxious.

Scale E - Emotional Symptoms – People scoring High on this scale tend to experience many distressing emotional symptoms when they are stressed and become very anxious.

Remember that even one symptom, physical or emotional, can be significant in daily functioning!

Signs of Stress Symptoms

Stress in My Work Life

Many different sources of stress occur in one's work-life.

Identify some of the situations at work that are currently triggering stress that leads to your anxiety. Place an X in the boxes of the situations that cause you stress and anxiety at or about work. Then write which symptoms you experience when they are happening. If the issue is with one or more person, identify the person by using a name-code (LIC = Likes Ice Cream).

Work Issues

- ☐ Boredom _____
- ☐ Burnout _____
- ☐ Change in supervisors _____
- ☐ Change in work load _____
- ☐ Changes in finances _____
- ☐ Frustration _____
- ☐ Interruptions _____
- ☐ Isolation _____
- ☐ Lack of meaningfulness _____
- ☐ Lack of support _____
- ☐ Looking for another job _____
- ☐ Loss of a job _____
- ☐ No appreciation _____
- ☐ No control of outcome _____
- ☐ Not enough or too many hours _____
- ☐ Not valued _____
- ☐ Overload _____
- ☐ Personal injury _____
- ☐ Physical environment _____
- ☐ Poor health issues _____
- ☐ Poor performance _____
- ☐ Poor preparation and training _____
- ☐ Retirement _____
- ☐ Safety concerns _____
- ☐ Skills do not match demands _____
- ☐ The "system" _____
- ☐ Too much or too little autonomy _____
- ☐ Uncertainty _____
- ☐ Underpaid _____
- ☐ Unequal treatment _____
- ☐ Unreasonable or unfair expectations _____
- ☐ Other _____

Being aware of anxiety triggers is the first step in managing them. Now that you have identified the source of stress, write about how you can reduce the stressors. *(Example: Talk with someone you trust, go out for lunch, take a walk during a break.)* **Continue writing on the reverse side of this page. Write about the stressor that is causing the most anxiety.**

Managing Intense Anxiety Workbook

Stress Associated With My Relationships

Many different sources of stress occur with one's varied relationships.

Identify some of the relationship issues that are currently triggering stress that leads to your anxiety. Place an X in the boxes of the situations that cause you stress and anxiety with any of your relationships. Then write which symptoms you experience when they are happening. If the issue is with one or more person, identify the person by using a name-code (MGF = My Good Friend).

Relationship Issues

- ☐ Abuse _____
- ☐ Anger _____
- ☐ Appreciation _____
- ☐ Availability _____
- ☐ Blame _____
- ☐ Breakup _____
- ☐ Child raising _____
- ☐ Children _____
- ☐ Clear or unclear messages _____
- ☐ Compatibility _____
- ☐ Consistency _____
- ☐ Control _____
- ☐ Crisis _____
- ☐ Death _____
- ☐ Empathy _____
- ☐ Family _____
- ☐ Finances _____
- ☐ Illness _____
- ☐ Infidelity _____
- ☐ In-laws _____
- ☐ Loyalty _____
- ☐ Partner _____
- ☐ Respect _____
- ☐ Sense of security _____
- ☐ Threats _____
- ☐ Trust _____
- ☐ Truthfulness _____
- ☐ Unmet needs _____
- ☐ Values _____
- ☐ Other _____
- ☐ Other _____

Being aware of anxiety triggers is the first step in managing them. Now that you have identified the relationships that are the sources of stress, write about how you can reduce the stressors. *(Example: Talk with someone you trust, lessen your time with this person, take a look at the Serenity Prayer.)* **Continue writing on the reverse side of this page. Write about the stressor that is causing the most anxiety.**

Signs of Stress Symptoms

My Stress Triggers

It is important to explore the stressful reaction triggers that create anxiety for you.

The following will help you examine what prompts stress in a variety of settings, Place an X in the boxes that apply to you. Then, in the space after each item you check, describe how the item applies to you. The area with the most boxes checked is your greatest source of stress triggers.

At Home
- ☐ When I am asked to do _____
- ☐ When someone _____
- ☐ When I feel like I'm _____
- ☐ When others don't _____
- ☐ When I think _____

At Home TOTAL = _____

At Work
- ☐ When I am asked to do _____
- ☐ When someone _____
- ☐ When I feel like I'm _____
- ☐ When others don't _____
- ☐ When I think _____

At Work TOTAL = _____

In Social Situations
- ☐ When I am asked to do _____
- ☐ When someone _____
- ☐ When I feel like I'm _____
- ☐ When others don't _____
- ☐ When I think _____

In Social Situations TOTAL = _____

In the Community
- ☐ When I am asked to do _____
- ☐ When someone _____
- ☐ When I feel like I'm _____
- ☐ When others don't _____
- ☐ When I think _____

In the Community TOTAL = _____

Managing Intense Anxiety Workbook

Thoughts about My Stress

Think back to a stressful situation that caused you to become intensely anxious. Journaling about that situation can help you better understand the situation and reduce your distress associated with it.

In the spaces that follow, journal about your stressful situation.

Describe the situation. _____
_____
_____
_____

How did you get into the situation? _____
_____
_____
_____

Who else plays a role in the situation? _____
_____
_____
_____

What happened? What did you do? _____
_____
_____
_____

What didn't you do? _____
_____
_____
_____

(Continued on the next page)

Signs of Stress Symptoms

Thoughts about My Stress (Continued)

What, if anything, could have been done differently? _____
_____
_____
_____

What stressed you out the most about the situation? _____
_____
_____
_____

How did you know it was resolved? _____
_____
_____
_____

What did you do after it was over? _____
_____
_____
_____

How have these stressful types of situations changed your life? _____
_____
_____
_____

(Continued on the next page)

Thoughts about My Stress (Continued)

How has it affected your present life? _____
_____
_____
_____

How has the event affected your future life? _____
_____
_____
_____

What was the worst aspect of the situation? _____
_____
_____
_____

Did you resolve your stress issue? _____ If not, how can you resolve your stress issue? _____
_____
_____
_____

What is something positive that has come out of the event? (example: relationships, new job, wisdom)
_____
_____
_____
_____
_____

Signs of Stress Symptoms

Picturing My Stress – NOW and THEN

We all have stress, and stress leads to anxiety. When that anxiety becomes intense, we need to be able to manage it.

One way to begin to gain control over stress and/or panic is to use your imagination, visualize what your stress looks or feels like, and draw a picture or a caricature of it.

What My Stress and Stressor(s) Look Like NOW

My Stress Looks Like	The Cause(s) of My Stress Looks Like

What I WOULD LIKE My Stress and Stressor(s) to Look Like

My Stress Looks Like	The Cause(s) of My Stress Looks Like

Managing Intense Anxiety Workbook

Worry-Work

Many people who experience intense anxiety tend to focus on the negatives in their lives. These negatives are often contained in the continuous running tape in their heads (self-talk).

In detail, describe the negative things you most often say to yourself, and then list the positives you *could* say instead. If you need more space, use a blank sheet of paper.

My Greatest Worry _____

Negative things I Say to Myself
   Example:
   My father had cancer and I worry that I will too.

Positive Things I Could Say to Myself
   I will do everything in my power to be healthy but if I do I get cancer, I will deal with it.

_____   _____

_____   _____

_____   _____

_____   _____

_____   _____

_____   _____

_____   _____

_____   _____

_____   _____

_____   _____

Signs of Stress Symptoms

Worry Self-Talk

The conversations that go on in your head can cause you tremendous amounts of anxiety.

**Answer the following questions to explore the type of negative self-talk you engage.
Circle the 3, 2, or 1 for each item (be honest!) and then add your scores to get your totals.**

	True	Sometimes True	NOT True
I worry all the time	3	2	1
I imagine the worst case scenario	3	2	1
I worry about what might happen	3	2	1
I worry about being embarrassed	3	2	1
I anticipate the worst	3	2	1

Worry Wart Scale = _____

I judge myself	3	2	1
I evaluate my behavior	3	2	1
I focus on my flaws	3	2	1
I compare myself with others	3	2	1
I ignore my positive qualities	3	2	1

Critic Scale = _____

I believe I'm not doing enough	3	2	1
I feel like I should be working harder	3	2	1
I hate making mistakes	3	2	1
I feel burned out pursuing my goals	3	2	1
I say "I should, or could, or would ..."	3	2	1

Perfectionist Scale = _____

The Scales on which you scored high, indicates the type of negative self-talk that happens in your head and heightens your anxiety. Transfer your totals below. The Range is 5 (not at all) to 15 (a lot!)

Worry Wart _____ Critic _____ Perfectionist _____

What are your observations about the results? _____

_____

_____

Managing Intense Anxiety Workbook

Recognizing Intense Anxiety Situations

It is important to be aware of and identify your high-anxiety situations; to attempt to avoid them, and if you can't, be prepared to deal with the stress that will arise.

What are your high-anxiety situations and how can you cope with them more effectively?

My High-Anxiety Situations	When I Encounter this Situation	How I React	How I Can Cope
Example: When asked to speak to large groups.	When my boss asks me to address the staff at work.	I get sweaty, begin to feel dizzy, and have trouble breathing.	Take deep breaths and limit the negative thoughts I have.

Which high-anxiety situations are particularly worrisome to you? _____
_____
_____

What steps can you take immediately to either avoid them or feel less stressed in that situation?
_____
_____
_____

Signs of Stress Symptoms

My Anxiety Symptoms

Anxiety symptoms can be both physical and emotional.

Take time to explore your anxiety symptoms, where they occur and what makes them better or worse?

Symptoms	Where They Occur	What Makes Them Worse	What Makes Them Better
Example: My heart beats very fast.	At work when my boss comes around.	When I do nothing about it.	It gets better if I take several deep breaths.

"A crust eaten in peace is better than a banquet partaken in anxiety!"
~ Aesop

What does the above quotation say to you and why is it important? _____

_____

_____

Managing Intense Anxiety Workbook

Anxiety Tension

People who have an intense level of anxiety are often unable to recognize tension and how they experience it.

This handout will help you explore how you experience tension when you are anxious.

External events leading to feelings of anxiety	Where in my body I feel the tension	Internal negative thoughts leading to feelings of anxiety	Internal positive thoughts leading to lessen feelings of anxiety
Example: Speaking in front of others at the next meeting.	I get an upset stomach and get light-headed.	They will not like my ideas.	I believe that my ideas are valuable and they will gain by hearing them.

What is one thing can you do to eliminate or reduce your feelings of anxiety? _____

_____

_____

_____

Signs of Stress Symptoms

Effects of Anxiety

Awareness of the effects of anxiety is the first step to overcoming it. It is important for you to think about the various ways that anxiety makes you feel in the settings you find yourself living and working in.

How does anxiety affect your day-to-day activities and interactions?

Setting	When I Become Anxious	How It Affects Me	How It Affects Others
Example: People	When there are a lot of people in the room talking.	I get jittery and can't sit still.	They become distracted by my movements.
People			
Work			
Home			
Community			
Other			

Managing Intense Anxiety Workbook

You Have Been Asked …

It is important to recognize the thoughts, feelings and emotions that accompany your stress that eventually lead to anxiety. One of the best ways to do this is to identify a situation and then practice letting go of the thoughts, emotions, and behaviors associated with this situation.

Write about something that you have been asked to do that always seems to heighten your anxiety, panic you, and/or stress you out! _____
_____
_____
_____

Take a deep breath … and … answer the following questions.

Notice any thoughts and name them. _____
_____
_____
_____
_____

Let them go.

Notice any emotions and name them. _____
_____
_____
_____
_____

Let them go.

Notice any behaviors and name them. _____
_____
_____
_____
_____

Let them go.

Signs of Stress Symptoms

Basic Anxiety Management Tools

There are some basic things you can do to help manage your anxiety.

Below, journal about lifestyle changes you can make to help reduce your anxiety.

EXERCISE REGULARLY: Attempt to get at least 30 minutes or more of aerobic activity each day.

My Exercise Habits _____

_____

_____

How I Can Do Better _____

_____

HEALTHY EATING HABITS: Eat plenty of complex carbohydrates such as whole grains, fruits, and vegetables. Limit sugars and alcohol in your diet.

My Eating Habits _____

_____

_____

How I Can Do Better _____

_____

SLEEP: Get enough sleep to maintain your emotional balance and reduce anxiety.

My Sleep Habits _____

_____

_____

How I Can Do Better _____

_____

RELAXATION: Engage in techniques that will relax you including yoga, meditation, and deep breathing.

My Relaxation Habits _____

_____

_____

How I Can Do Better _____

_____

Managing Intense Anxiety Workbook

My Coping Strategies

It is important that you learn basic techniques for coping with and managing your stress. By doing so, you will reduce the amounts of anxiety that you experience.

Think back over the past week, and describe which types of coping mechanisms you used, how effective they were, and the end result. Complete this table to identify effective stress-management techniques.

Techniques	I Tried and Liked It. Why I Like It.	I Have Not Tried It. Why I Haven't.	I Tried and Do Not Like it. Why Not?
Example: *Relaxation.*	When I feel stress, I immediately look for a quiet place to close my eyes and simply focus on my breath until I calm down. I like it because it is easy to do.	I have not tried it because I didn't know how to go about it.	I don't know how to make this work because I can't always find a quiet, safe place.
Relaxation – *Find a quiet place to relax, meditate, do yoga, listen to soothing music, draw, guided imagery, write.*			
Breathing – *Take time to simply breathe. Take deep breaths in through your nose and breathe out through your mouth.*			
Prescribed Meds – *Be sure that you have taken your medications as prescribed by a physician.*			
Support – *Confide in and talk with trusted friends and family and/or a therapist about your stress and anxiety.*			
Distract Myself – *Find productive, relaxing, and enjoyable ways, to take your mind off your anxiety.*			
Other			

Signs of Stress Symptoms

Quick Meditation

When you begin to experience signs of stress and start to feel anxiety, it can be very helpful to do a quick meditation to reduce the stress quickly and easily. Meditation is easy and helps you relax, become calm, and stop the thoughts about the event from flooding back into your consciousness.

Here is the *Quick Meditation* process:

1. Right now, think of a place that is calming to you, such as a clearing in a forest, a prime spot on a beach, a balcony on a cruise, etc.

2. With this image in your mind, gently close your eyes and focus on this image. If you have thoughts (other than your calm place), acknowledge them and let them go.

3. After one minute, open your eyes.

How do you feel right now? _____

_____

_____

What thoughts popped back into your head? _____

_____

_____

How does your stress feel now? _____

_____

_____

How does your anxiety feel now?_____

_____

_____

**Keep practicing this daily for five to ten minutes,
and you will notice your anxiety becoming less prominent.**

Managing Intense Anxiety Workbook

MY KRYPTONITE

Superman could do just about anything and was not afraid of anything. However, even Superman had his kryptonite. For Superman, kryptonite was a mineral from the planet Krypton that drained Superman of his strength.

On the minerals below, write about various aspects of your kryptonite, or those things that take your strength away and fill you with anxiety. For example, if you are afraid to speak in public, you might write about fear of how people will evaluate you, how you might embarrass yourself, others laughing at you, etc.

My kryptonite is …

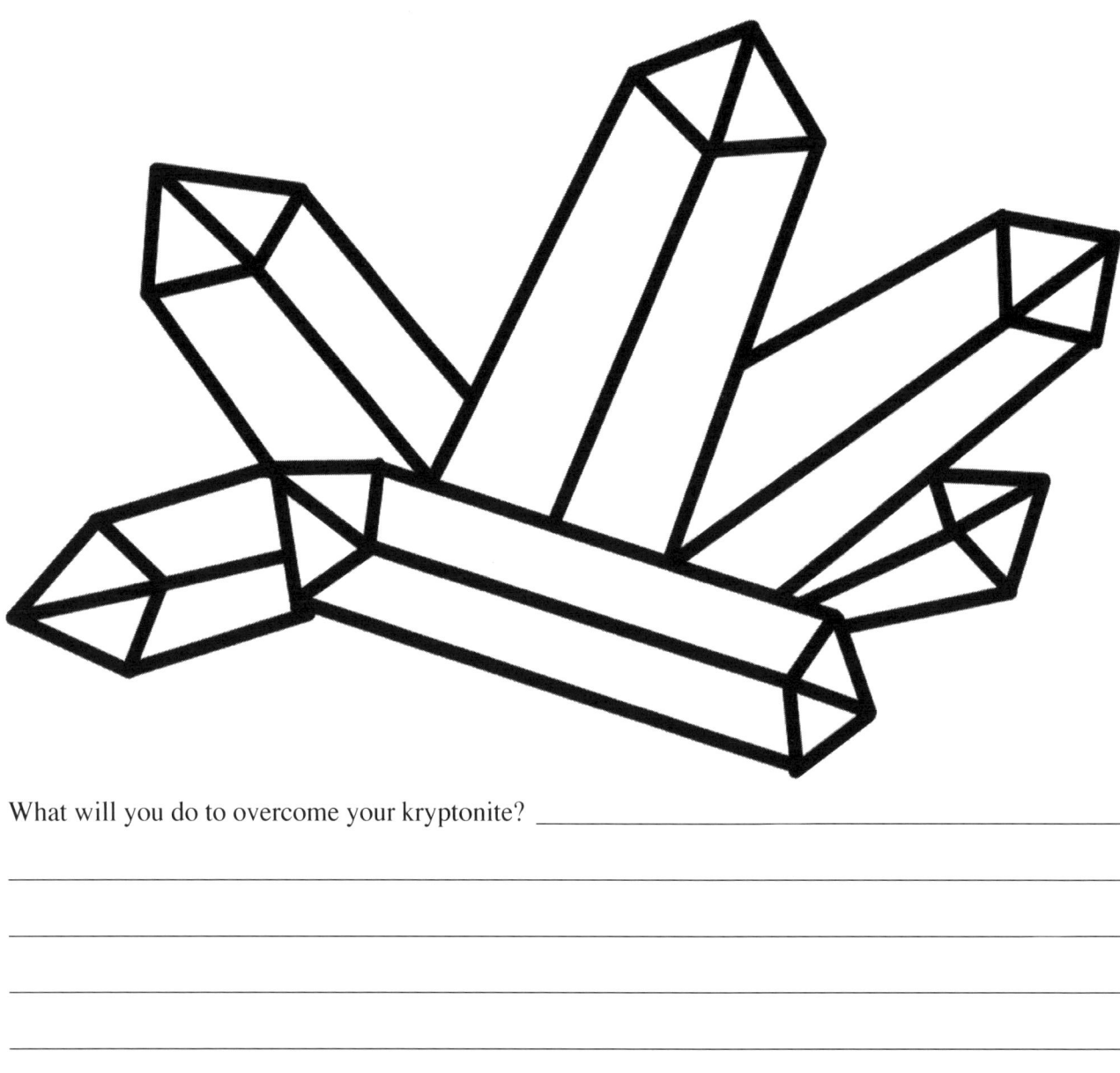

What will you do to overcome your kryptonite? _____

_____

_____

_____

_____

MODULE II

Need for Control

Grant me the serenity …
to accept the people I cannot
change, the courage to
change the one I can, and
the wisdom to know it's me.

~ ***Adaptation of The Serenity Prayer***

Name _____

Date _____

Module II – Take-Away Skills

We have included skills for most of the handouts in each Module, *Conditions and Behavior* (1), *Frequency and Duration* (2), and/or *Accomplishment* (3) statements for each activity may be used in educational and/or treatment planning, and also used to measure progress toward goals. These Take-Away skills promote real life outcomes and behavioral changes. Feel free to add additional skills for each activity.

Examples

1. **Conditions and Behavior** – a skill or healthy habit to replace a previous less effective behavior/habit.
   - Now, I … *(less effective or undesired behavior)*
     when I … *(when do I do this?)*.
     Instead I will … *(more effective or desired new behavior)* in ___ out of ___ opportunities.
2. **Frequency and Duration** – a skill or healthy habit not necessarily tied to a condition or previous behavior.
   - I will *(describe the behavior)* ___ times per ___.
3. **Accomplishment** – an outcome that is a one-time accomplishment.
   - I will *(describe the accomplishment)* by ___ *(date)*.

Take-Away Skills Examples

Control or Not? 48
Conditions and Behavior
- Now, I … *feel overwhelmed and shut down*
  when … *there is a change in my routine at work.*
  Instead I will … *recognize what I can control in the situation and accept what I cannot, in 3 out of 3 opportunities.*
- Now, I … *tell my kids "no" out of worry*
  when … *they ask to do something by themselves.*
  Instead I will … *stop and determine if my thought is rational or irrational before answering, 4 out of 4 opportunities.*

Changes in My Life 49
Frequency and Duration
- I will … *complete the Changes in My Life activity to reframe the change in a positive light 1 time every week for 1 month.*

Go to Your Fears 51
Conditions and Behavior
- Now, I … *avoid going to the dentist out of fear*
  when … *I have a toothache.*
  Instead I will … *call and schedule an appointment, 3 out of 3 opportunities.*

Take-Away Skills Examples *(Continued)*

Taking Action to Reduce Anxiety 53
    Accomplishment
- *I will set one long-term goal for my future by the end of the week.*
- *I will identify three short-term goals as steps toward reaching my long-term goal, by the March 31st.*
- *I will go to the dentist by the end of the month.*

    Frequency and Duration
- *I will … complete one short-term goal off of my list, 1 time every week for 1 month.*

Over and Over and Over Again! 54
    Conditions and Behavior
- Now, I … *ruminate on negative thoughts*
  when I … *have to talk to my boss.*
  Instead I will … *complete the Hocus-Focus steps, 4 out of 4 opportunities.*

What's the Worst Thing? 56
    Conditions and Behavior
- Now, I … *worry excessively*
  when I … *think about an upcoming event I have to attend.*
  Instead I will … *think about the worst thing that could happen to reduce my anxiety, 4 out of 4 opportunities.*

From a Self-Fulfilling Prophecy to Imagining the Best 57
    Conditions and Behavior
- Now, I … *psych myself out*
  when I … *am thinking about going to a gathering with people I do not know.*
  Instead I will … *think about all of the good things that will happen there, 4 out of 4 opportunities.*

Staying in the Present 58
    Conditions and Behavior
- Now, I … *experience my mind wandering*
  when I … *think about all of the things that could go wrong in my relationship.*
  Instead I will … *bring my attention back to the word "peace" 4 out of 4 opportunities.*

Relaxing Your Body 60
    Frequency and Duration
- *I will … complete a Body Scan deep breathing exercise 1 time a day for 2 weeks.*
- *I will … practice Total-Body Relaxation 1 time a day for a week.*

Mindfulness 61
    Frequency and Duration
- *I will … practice a mindfulness exercise for 15 minutes 1 time a day for 1 week.*
- *I will … journal about the mindfulness exercise after practicing it 1 time a day for a week.*

Managing Intense Anxiety Workbook

Need for Control Scale
Introduction and Directions

The need for control is often a reaction to the fear of losing control. People who feel the need for control are typically afraid of being in unpredictable situations, feeling vulnerable, and/or living with uncertainty. People who feel this need for control often become very anxious when control eludes them.

This assessment contains 18 statements designed to help you explore the ways in which you become anxious because of the need to feel in control of your environment. Read each of the statements and decide whether the statement describes you or not. If the statement does describe you, circle the number in the YES column next to that item. If the statement does not describe you, circle the number in the NO column next to that item. Do not worry about the numbers for now.

In the following example, the circled 2 indicates the statement does not describe the person completing the inventory

	YES	NO
1. I need to be in control	1	2

This is not a test. Since there are no right or wrong answers, do not spend too much time thinking about your answers. Be sure to respond to every statement.

(Turn to the next page and begin.)

Managing Intense Anxiety Workbook

Need for Control Scale

	YES	NO
I need to be in control	2	1
I worry about what others think of me	2	1
I want to control everything that happens to me	2	1
It's hard for me to trust that others will do things correctly	2	1
I often feel powerless and don't like it	2	1
I don't like feeling vulnerable	2	1

Scale V = _____

I worry about things occurring in the world	2	1
I worry about being in new situations	2	1
I lack self-confidence around people I don't know	2	1
I worry about making the wrong decisions	2	1
I worry in situations in which I do not feel in control	2	1
I worry when things change	2	1

Scale U = _____

I worry about the unknown	2	1
I usually imagine the worst	2	1
I need to feel in control to feel safe	2	1
I worry when I don't know what's going to happen	2	1
I worry about the future	2	1
I worry about unfamiliar situations	2	1

Scale S = _____

Go to the Scoring Directions

Need for Control Scale
Scoring Directions

The *Need for Control Scale* you just completed is designed to measure how a lack of control bothers you. For each of the sections on the previous page, count the scores you circled. Put that total on the line marked TOTAL at the end of each section.

Then, transfer your total to the space below:

        V **Vulnerable Total**   = _____

        U **Uncertainly Total**   = _____

        S **Situational Total**   = _____

Add your scores together for your Grand Total. _____

Profile Interpretation

Individual Score	Grand Total	Result	Indications
6 – 7	18 – 23	Low	Low scores indicate that you are not experiencing much anxiety due to the need for control. Complete the following exercises to continue.
8 – 10	24 – 30	Moderate	Medium scores indicate that you are experiencing some anxiety due to the need for control. Complete the following exercises to continue.
11 – 12	31 – 36	High	High scores indicate that you are experiencing a great deal of anxiety due to the need for control. Complete the following exercises to continue.

Scale Descriptions

Vulnerable – People scoring High on this scale become anxious because they do not trust others, always need to be in control of their environment, and hate to feel vulnerable and powerless.

Uncertainty – People scoring High on this scale tend to worry about the unknown, worry about the future, and do not feel safe if they are not in complete control of their lives.

Situational – People scoring High on this scale do not like to experience change, they get anxious when confronted with new situations, and worry about problems occurring in the world.

GRAND TOTAL – High scores on all three scales indicate that the person tends to become very anxious and full of worry when they do not feel in control of their lives or their environment. They do not like to feel vulnerable or powerless, dislike and face new situations, and constantly worry about the future.

Managing Intense Anxiety Workbook

Control or Not?

It is important to examine the areas in your life that you can control and those you cannot control.

Identify what you cannot control and what you can control in the various areas in your life.

Areas of My Life	What I Cannot Control	What I Can Control
Example: At Home.	I cannot control the late hours my husband needs to work.	I can control the things I need to do to feel safe..
At Home		
Educationally		
In the Community		
In My Personal Life		
In My Social Life		
At Work		
Other		

In which areas of your life do you have the ability to control? _____
_____
_____

How can you let go of the things you cannot control. _____
_____
_____

Need for Control

Changes in My Life

Change is anxiety-producing for some people. Change is stepping into the unknown and can increase the amounts of stress and anxiety you experience. What is changing in your life?

Write about these changes and explore how your perceptions affect your feelings about the change.

A Change In My Life	Is This Change in My Control? Why or why not?	Is This Change Comfortable for Me? Why?	Is This Change Uncomfortable for Me? Why?	How I Can Look at This Change in a Positive Light
Example: A breakup.	Not really. I can't make my partner get help.	Yes – I don't want my children to see abuse and think it's okay.	Yes – I still love my partner.	My children will be better off in the long run, and so will I.

Why is the unknown so scary? _____

_____

_____

My "IF" Fears

Fears are often triggered because of a lack of control over one's environment. One wonders, *What if this happens?* or *What if that happens?* Fears can be rational or irrational.
What are your "IF" fears? How are they interfering with your ability to lead a satisfying life?

In the spaces that follow, list your fears and how they are related to a lack of control.

My "IF" Fears	Rational or Irrational	How They are Tied to a Lack of Control	What I Can Do To Overcome These Fears
Example: My children getting into a car accident.	Irrational – they are all good drivers.	I still want to protect them.	Remind myself that they are responsible, and know how to be careful and safe.

Need for Control

Go to Your Fears

> *Go to your fears, sit with them, stare at them. Your fears are your friend; their only job is to show you undeveloped parts of yourself that you need to cultivate to live a happy life. The more you do the things you're most afraid of doing, the more life opens up. Embrace your fears and they will embrace you.*
>
> **~ Jackson Kiddard**

What does this quotation say to you? _____

_____

_____

_____

What are your fears? _____

_____

_____

_____

When have you done things you were afraid of doing? _____

_____

_____

_____

How did it work out, and how could it have worked out differently? _____

_____

_____

_____

Which fear are you ready to embrace? _____

_____

_____

_____

Doodling

Doodling is an excellent way for you to unleash the power of self-expression.

You do not need to be an artist to doodle. You are the only one who needs to know what the doodle represents. Doodling is simply drawing something without thinking a lot about it. It is designed to help you put your left brain (your logical brain) on hold while you use your right brain (the creative part of your brain). Doodles can be silly designs, drawings, icons, abstract shapes, lines, or intermittent words.

I wish I had more control over …	Vulnerability looks like …

Uncertainty looks like …	The future looks like …

Need for Control

Taking Action to Reduce Anxiety

Taking action (rather than dwelling on what might happen) can reduce your feelings of powerlessness.

What is a long-term goal that will help you to feel less anxious about the future?
Write that long-term goal below, and then in the table below, set several smaller goals to achieve this long-term goal. Be as specific as you possibly can be.

My Long-Term Goal: _____

My Short-Term Goals in Order to Reach My Long Term-Goal	What I Can do To Achieve This Short-Term Goal	How It Will Contribute to My Long-Term Goal
1.		
2.		
3.		
4.		
5.		

If you have more than 5 short term goals, continue on the back of the page.

Managing Intense Anxiety Workbook

Over and Over and Over Again!

Often, people who are very anxious have thoughts, images, or impulses, that occur over and over again, and things that feel outside of their control. They are usually intense and uncomfortable.

Write about them below.

Thoughts, Images, and Impulses that Repeat Over and Over Again	When I Have These Thoughts	How These Thoughts Affect Me

If you need more space, please use the reverse side of this handout.

Need for Control

Hocus-Focus

If you need more space, please use the reverse side of this handout.

People with intense anxiety often have repeating thoughts that keep them focused on their thinking rather than actions.

Below are a set of magical steps that you can take to dramatically reduce your feelings of anxiety by focusing on your behaviors and not your thoughts.

Describe a situation in which you had obtrusive, repeating thoughts: _____

_____

_____

In the space next to each magic wand below, write how you could refocus your attention.

Step 1: Recognize and re-label intrusive thoughts that tell you that something is wrong:

Step 2: Focus your attention on something else:

Step 3: Pay attention and focus on your next behaviors and not on your thoughts:

What's the Worst Thing?

When you are worrying, try asking yourself, *What's the worst thing that can happen?* **Often people find out that the worst thing isn't really that bad, and often the worst thing doesn't happen!**

Think about a time lately when you felt anxious about something that might happen in the future.

What was the situation? _____

_____

_____

_____

When you think about it, what emotions did you experience? _____

_____

_____

_____

How did you experience the anxiety in your body? _____

_____

_____

_____

What was the worst thing that could have happened in this situation? _____

_____

_____

_____

What did happen? _____

_____

_____

_____

In the future, ask yourself these questions and focus on the positive? It IS POSSIBLE that it will turn out okay. Staying positive helps! _____

_____

_____

_____

Need for Control

From a Self-Fulfilling Prophecy to Imagining the Best

When you focus on everything that can go wrong, you are putting into motion a self-fulfilling prophecy for yourself. In other words, when you imagine how something in the future will be bad or go wrong, it possibly will! For this activity, let's turn that around.

Think about an event that you have coming up in the future and write about all of the good things that will happen at this event. Be creative!

The event: _____

_____

_____

_____

_____

The good things that can happen (be specific): _____

_____

_____

_____

_____

Steps I need to take to make sure good things will happen (be specific): _____

_____

_____

_____

_____

Now LET GO of the negative thinking. How can I do that? _____

_____

_____

_____

_____

Managing Intense Anxiety Workbook

Staying in the Present

Paying attention and attending to whatever you are doing in the present is one of the best ways to reduce anxiety related to the unknown future. Being attentive can lessen the impact and help you to step back from thoughts and feelings about the future or the past.

Let's practice mindfulness now.
1. Look around you and focus on something of interest to you.
2. Concentrate on the object.
3. Each time your mind begins to wander from the object, bring it back to full attention.
4. Do this for several minutes.
5. Then journal about the following questions.

How did you feel during the activity? _____
_____
_____

Did you have difficulty attending to the object? If so, why? _____
_____
_____
_____

What did you notice about your thoughts as you mindfully attended to the object? _____
_____
_____
_____

How can this help you? _____
_____
_____
_____

Need for Control

Deep Breathing

> *When you own your breath, nobody can steal your peace.*
> ~ **Author Unknown**

Deep breathing can help reduce your anxiety the following ways:
- Reduces hyperventilation when you encounter stressors
- Helps you feel calm
- Helps you reduce anxiety quickly
- Reduces everyday stress
- Reduce panic and anxiety

1. Scan your body and identify the parts of your body where you are experiencing your anxiety. List those parts of your body: _____
   _____

2. Next, inhale slowly through your nose until you see your abdomen rising. Hold this breath for five seconds.

3. Then, exhale through your mouth slowly, pushing all of the air out. Do this again five times until you feel more relaxed.

How can you use this technique when you are feeling anxious? _____
_____
_____

How do you think this technique might help you? _____
_____
_____

How do you think this technique would not help you? _____
_____
_____

Relaxing Your Body

Anxiety manifests itself through physical symptoms in your body. These physical symptoms often reinforce your anxiety-producing thoughts and feelings. Total-Body Relaxation (often called Progressive Muscle Relaxation) is a simple technique used to stop anxiety by relaxing all of the muscles throughout your body one group at a time.

Read through the following script several times before you attempt to do this exercise.

1. *Take a few deep breaths, and begin to relax.*
2. *Get comfortable and put aside all of your worries.*
3. *Let each part of your body begin to relax … starting with your feet.*
4. *Imagine your feet relaxing as all of your tension begins to fade away.*
5. *Imagine the relaxation moving up into your calves and thighs … feel them beginning to relax.*
6. *Allow the relaxation to move into your waist.*
7. *Continue now to let the relaxation move into your hips and stomach.*
8. *Your entire body from the waist down is now completely relaxed.*
9. *Let go of any strain and discomfort you might feel.*
10. *Allow the relaxation to move into your chest until your chest feels completely relaxed.*
11. *Just enjoy the feeling of complete relaxation.*
12. *Continue to let the relaxation move through the muscles of your shoulders, then spread down into your upper arms, into your elbows, and finally all the way down to your wrists and hands.*
13. *Put aside all of your worries.*
14. *Let yourself be totally present in the moment and let yourself relax more and more. Let all the muscles in your neck unwind and let the relaxation move into your chin and jaws.*
15. *Feel the tension around your eyes flow away as the relaxation moves throughout your face and head.*
16. *Feel your forehead relax and your entire head beginning to feel lighter.*
17. *Let yourself drift deeper and deeper into relaxation and peace.*

After you have read the above paragraph several times, find a quiet location where you can practice Total-Body Relaxation.

- Assume a comfortable position in a chair.
- Take off your jewelry and glasses so that you are totally free.
- Try to let the relaxation happen without having to force it.
- If during the relaxation you lose concentration, don't be concerned - just begin again.

Need for Control

Mindfulness

Mindfulness can help you to live in the moment and worry less about the unknowns. People who feel like they need control can experience that feeling by being mindful of the present and accepting it without judgment.

Try these activities to help develop mindfulness. Journal about your experience.

Mindfulness Meditation – For this activity, sit quietly and focus on your natural breathing movements. Now begin to focus on the word peace and repeat it silently to yourself with each breath. Allow thoughts to come and go by simply returning to focus on the word peace. Do this for two minutes. What was this experience like for you? _____

_____
_____
_____
_____
_____
_____
_____

Body Mindfulness – For this activity, sit quietly and focus on your subtle bodily changes (eye twitching, foot tingling, etc.). Scan your body from head to toe, noting any sensations. Dismiss any thoughts, acknowledge any sensations and then return to your scanning. Do this for two minutes. What was this experience like for you? _____

_____
_____
_____
_____
_____
_____
_____

Which did you like best and why? _____
_____

Managing Intense Anxiety Workbook

Mindfulness Journaling

Mindfulness is being aware of the present moment and not allowing yourself to be pulled into the past or the future.

Complete the activity and then journal about your results.

Take a minute right now to focus all of your attention on your breathing. Keep your eyes open and just breathe normally. Be aware of when your mind begins to wander and return your attention to your breath when this happens. Journal about your experience:

How difficult was it to keep your mind on your breathing? _____
_____
_____
_____

What did you find your mind doing? _____
_____
_____
_____

What thoughts did you have about the past? _____
_____
_____
_____

What thoughts did you have about the future? _____
_____
_____
_____

Use this exercise during the day to bring your attention back to the present to restore peace and calm.

MODULE III

Social Approval

Most fears of rejection rest on the desire for approval from other people. Don't base your self-esteem on their opinions.

~ Harvey Mackay

Name _____

Date _____

Module III – Take-Away Skills

We have included skills for most of the handouts in each Module, *Conditions and Behavior* (1), *Frequency and Duration* (2), and/or *Accomplishment* (3) statements for each activity may be used in educational and/or treatment planning, and also used to measure progress toward goals. These Take-Away skills promote real life outcomes and behavioral changes. Feel free to add additional skills for each activity.

Examples

1. **Conditions and Behavior** – a skill or healthy habit to replace a previous less effective behavior/habit.
   - Now, I … *(less effective or undesired behavior)*
     when I … *(when do I do this?)*.
     Instead I will … *(more effective or desired new behavior)* in ___ out of ___ opportunities.
2. **Frequency and Duration** – a skill or healthy habit not necessarily tied to a condition or previous behavior.
   - I will *(describe the behavior)* _____ times per _____.
3. **Accomplishment** – an outcome that is a one-time accomplishment.
   - I will *(describe the accomplishment)* by _____ *(date)*.

Take-Away Skills Examples

People with Whom I Feel Anxious 71
Conditions and Behavior
- Now, I … *avoid the lunchroom*
  when … *my boss is in there*.
  Instead I will … *go to the lunchroom at lunchtime, regardless whether or not my boss is in there, 5 out of 5 opportunities*.

Need for Approval 75
Conditions and Behavior
- Now, I … *react defensively*
  when I … *am given negative feedback*.
  Instead I will … *accept the criticism 4 out of 4 times*.
- Now, I … *avoid asking questions*
  when I … *am afraid other people will think I am stupid*.
  Instead I will … *ask for clarification when I do not understand, 4 out of 4 opportunities*.

Take-Away Skills Examples *(Continued)*

I'm Good Enough 77
   Accomplishment
   - *I will attend a new club meeting by the end of the month.*
   - *I will take one community education class by the end the year.*

   Conditions and Behavior
   - Now, I ... *become tense*
     when ... *someone is looking at me.*
     Instead, I will. . . *use deep breathing to remain calm, 4 out of 4 opportunities.*
   - Now, I ... *"beat myself up"*
     when I ... *commit a social blunder.*
     Instead, I will ... *use a self-soothing technique 4 out of 4 opportunities.*
   - Now, I ... *avoid going to a support group*
     when I ... *don't know anyone.*
     Instead I will ... *use deep breathing and attend the event, 4 out of 4 opportunities.*

Challenging Negative Thinking 79
   Conditions and Behavior
   - Now, I ... *automatically say "no" out of fear*
     when ... *someone asks me out on a date.*
     Instead I will ... *stop and determine if it is my anxiety 'talking' before making a decision, 4 out of 4 opportunities.*

Positive Self-Talk Scripts 80
   Conditions and Behavior
   - Now, I ... *become short of breath*
     when I ... *am anticipating going to a community event.*
     Instead I will ... *rehearse a positive self-talk script, 4 out of 4 opportunities.*

Meet New People 81
   Frequency and Duration
   - *I will try out a new church 2 times every month for 2 months.*
   - *I will volunteer at the local animal shelter 1 time a week for 1 month.*

Accepting Myself 83
   Conditions and Behavior
   - Now, I ... *say "yes" to someone*
     when I ... *feel a need to be validated.*
     Instead I will ... *determine what is best for me before making a decision, 4 out of 4 opportunities.*

Social Approval

Social Approval Scale
Introduction and Directions

People who have social concerns and/or experience social anxiety often worry about being scrutinized, judged, disliked, and/or evaluated negatively, or the center of attention. They feel the need for social approval and fear saying or doing something embarrassing, or making mistakes.

This assessment contains 24 statements designed to help you explore the level of how much you need social approval and the degree to which a lack of social approval creates anxiety for you. Read each of the statements and decide whether the statement describes you or not, in ways you react in social situations.

If the statement does describe you, circle the number in the YES column next to that item. If the statement does not describe you, circle the number in the NO column next to that item.

In social situations …	YES	NO
I worry about how others perceive me	(2)	1

This is not a test. Since there are no right or wrong answers, do not spend too much time thinking about your answers. Be sure to respond to every statement.

(Turn to the next page and begin.)

Need for Control Scale

In social situations …

	YES	NO
I always believe I perform poorly	2	1
I am unable to work well because of my social anxiety	2	1
I avoid large groups	2	1
I become very anxious when involved in a social situation	2	1
I believe the opinions of others are more important than mine	2	1
I am concerned about looking foolish to others	2	1
I don't like meeting people I don't know	2	1
I don't like to socialize with people who are not as smart as I am	2	1
I do not want to hear negative feedback	2	1
I fear social situations	2	1
I feel uncomfortable expressing opinions that are different from others	2	1
I find that I am bothered when others' opinions are contrary to mine	2	1
I get tense if someone is looking at me	2	1
I get upset if I think someone has an unfavorable impression of me	2	1
I get upset when I commit a social blunder	2	1
I often think about what will happen before I do anything	2	1
I react poorly when people disapprove of me	2	1
I'm afraid that people will find fault with me	2	1
I say something and then I feel embarrassed	2	1
I usually feel as if I am being judged by others	2	1
I worry about how others perceive me	2	1
I worry about what others know about me	2	1
I worry when people of authority are around	2	1
I'm afraid of acting in a way that I will be humiliated	2	1

Total = _____

Go to the Scoring Directions

Need for Control Scale
Scoring Directions

The *Social Approval Scale* you just completed is designed to measure how much you need social approval from others in any social situation. Count the scores you circled on the previous page. Then, put that total on the line marked TOTAL at the end of the scale.

Then, transfer your total to the space below:

Social Approval Scale = _____

Profile Interpretation

Score Total	Result	Indications
24 – 31	Low	Low scores indicate that you do not have much of a need for social approval from others.
32 – 40	Moderate	Moderate scores indicate that you have some need for social approval from others.
41 – 48	High	High scores indicate that you have a great need for social approval from others.

Scale Descriptions

People scoring High on this scale tend to worry about other people watching them and judging them, worry about the opinions of others, and are very worried about looking foolish to other people. They worry about meeting new people, being in any social situation, and being judged by people in authority.

Managing Intense Anxiety Workbook

Events Where I Feel Anxious

Make a list of the social events in which you feel you might have intense anxiety or panic. These events can be at home, in the workplace, or anywhere.

Answer the following questions to identify how much effort you are making to avoid social events that might cause you anxiety.

Social Events I Avoid	Why I Avoid Them	What I Miss or Lose by Avoiding Them
Example: Dinner parties.	Too many people watching me and judging what I say.	I miss meeting new people, and I insult the person who invited me.

Which events are the easiest to avoid? When is it most difficult? Why? _____

_____

_____

_____

Social Approval

People with Whom I Feel Anxious

Being around certain people can also cause anxiety. Make a list of the people in whose presence, you begin to feel anxious, panicky, or worried. These people can be at home, in the workplace, or anywhere.

Answer the following questions to identify how much effort you are exerting to avoid the people who make you anxious.

People I Avoid	Why I Avoid Them	What I Miss or Lose by Avoiding This Person
Example: My boss when I'm in the lunch room.	I fear he is not happy with my performance and will tell me.	Opportunities to grow at work and let my boss know I'm doing a great job!

Which events are the easiest to avoid? When is it most difficult? Why? _____
_____
_____

Which are the most difficult? Why? _____
_____
_____

Managing Intense Anxiety Workbook

Situations Where I Feel Anxious

Make a list of the situations in which you have been very anxious, panicked, or worried. These situations can be at home, in the workplace, or anywhere.

Answer the following questions to identify how much effort you are exerting to avoid the situations that cause you to feel anxiety.

People I Avoid	Why I Avoid Them	What I Miss by Avoiding This Situation
Example: A situation in which I am asked to share something with a group of people I do not know.	I feel like other people are always judging me.	Being in social situations where I could meet new people and share valuable opinions or information.

Which situation is the easiest to avoid? Why? _____
_____
_____

Which situation is the most difficult? Why? _____
_____
_____

Ways I Avoid Social Situations

Many people will go to extreme lengths to avoid social situations.

Think about some of the things you do to not be in certain social situations and complete the table below.

Ways I Avoid Social Situations	How I Do This	The Positive and/or Negative Results of Avoidance
Example: Remove myself from the situation.	I will not accept dinner invitations when there are too many people with whom to talk.	I don't get anxious, but on the other hand, I miss out on getting to know other people.
Remove myself from the situation.		
Avoid attention to myself.		
Use substances to be more social.		
Over-prepare and rehearse.		
Think about other things.		
Focus on others, not myself.		
Other		

Which is your primary method for avoiding social situations? What steps will you now take to stop avoiding social situations as much? _____

_____

Social Approval

Social Situation Realities

People often over-exaggerate the negative impact of social situations in which they find themselves. It is important to carefully examine how you interact and perform in social situations.

Think of a social situation in which you recently found yourself, and answer the questions.

The Situation: _____
_____
_____

What was your concern about what might happen? _____
_____
_____
_____

Did it happen? _____
_____
_____
_____

If so, what was the worst thing about it? _____
_____
_____
_____

If not, what actually happened? _____
_____
_____
_____

Why were you so concerned about it? _____
_____
_____
_____

Social Approval

Need for Approval

People who experience a great deal of anxiety, especially in social situations, often feel a tremendous need for approval. In the spaces that follow, explore your need for approval from others in social situations.

Think about how you think, feel, and act when other people are present.

Why I Need Approval	What I Avoid	The Effect This Has on Me
Example: I want to be liked by everyone.	I avoid situations in which I might disagree with others.	I am always on guard.
I want to be liked by everyone.		
I seek positive feedback from others.		
I don't have the confidence I need.		
I believe that others are better than I am.		
I feel different from other people.		
I depend on others for my self-worth.		
Other		
Other		

Why do you think you feel this way? Give an example. _____

_____

_____

Validation

Although everyone likes to be validated, it is helpful to let go of the notion of needing validation for who you are as a person or for your life choices. Now is the time to believe you are good enough and to stop needing other people to validate this fact.

For the following activity, answer each of the sentence starters below.

The people I want to validate my choices, or who I am, are …

These people are important because …

The choices I have made because of the need for validation include …

I want _____ to say I'm okay because …

Upcoming choices I want to make because they are best for me include …

I will ensure that I am making decisions that are best for me by…

> *When we consistently suppress and distrust our intuitive knowingness, looking instead for authority, validation, and approval from others, we give our personal power away.*
>
> **~ Shakti Gawain**

Social Approval

I'm Good Enough!

People who feel anxiety associated with looking good in the eyes of others often feel as if whatever they do is not enough. This belief is a negative, internal statement that you might be telling yourself often.

In the table that follows, identify those people whom you believe are constantly judging you negatively. This may be one person or several people, someone whose name you know or do not know - a leader, a group, another culture, etc.

Ways I Think People Perceive Me	The Reality About Me	How I Can Think About This
Example: I think my partner thinks I'm lazy because I take Saturday off to nurture myself.	I work hard during the week and need to nurture myself on Saturdays.	I need to do what I need to do. I can explain it to my partner and then, let my partner think whatever.

What steps can you take to let go and accept that what you think about yourself is what is most important. _____

_____

_____

_____

Rejection, Abandonment, and Disapproval

Many people who have problems with social anxiety have underlying fears of rejection, abandonment, and disapproval.

Identify three of your fears and answer the questions below to explore the levels of each of them. Place an X on the lines below of each of your fears.

MY FEAR: _____

0_____**10**
(Not Very Fearful)   *(Very Fearful)*

How does this fear manifest itself in your daily life? _____

_____

_____

_____

MY FEAR: _____

0_____**10**
(Not Very Fearful)   *(Very Fearful)*

How does this fear manifest itself in your daily life? _____

_____

_____

_____

MY FEAR: _____

0_____**10**
(Not Very Fearful)   *(Very Fearful)*

How does this fear manifest itself in your daily life? _____

_____

_____

_____

Social Approval

Challenge Negative Thinking

People who suffer from social anxiety most often experience a wide variety of negative thoughts that keep repeating in their heads.

Think about a social situation in which you find yourself experiencing intense anxiety.

List that social situation: _____

_____

_____

On the left-hand side, identify some of the negative thoughts that build toward your anxiety. Then, on the right-hand side, analyze and challenge your negative thoughts.

Negative Thoughts	**Analyze and Challenge These Thoughts**

Managing Intense Anxiety Workbook

Positive Self-Talk Scripts

One aspect of people who need social approval is that they get a negative thought in their head and then other negative thoughts build on the original one until it accumulates and the person shuts down.

For the following activity, identify which negative thought often begins your negative thinking in a social situation and then list other thoughts that follow:

> Original Thought:
>
> Other Thoughts That Follow:

Now list some positive thoughts that you could immediately use to counteract your negative thoughts from building.

> Original Thought:
>
> Other Thoughts That Follow:

Social Approval

Meet New People

People with social approval and social anxiety issues often have a difficult time meeting new people and developing new relationships.

What are some ways you can get involved in activities to meet new people in a safe way?

Places to Meet New People	How I Can Accomplish This	Advantages
Example: At work.	Go to lunch with new people.	Make friends with colleagues in other areas of the company.
Work		
Clubs		
Organizations		
Volunteer		
Classes		
Athletic Events		
Religious/Spiritual Activites		
Artistic Events		
Social Media		
Other		

Which options seems to be the best for you? Why? _____

_____

_____

Self-Appreciation

Many people seek approval from others because they do not appreciate themselves enough. You need to take time to appreciate yourself.

In the spaces that follow write words, doodle, or attach cutouts from magazines about some of the things you appreciate about yourself and how you show this appreciation.

I appreciate my …	I appreciate how I …

I appreciate that I am …	I show my appreciation for who I am by …

Now share your work with others.

Accepting Myself

A primary step to overcoming your need for social approval is to accept yourself for who you are and not try to be someone or something else.

In the spaces that follow, identify how you accept yourself for who you are.

Situations	Ways I Accept Myself	How I Am Able to Use This Aspect of Myself
Example: At work.	*I know I am a great "team player."*	*I can assert myself to develop good work relationships and collaboration.*
At Work		
At Home		
In My Community		
In Social Situations		
Classes		
Other		
Other		

MODULE IV

Perfectionism

Perfectionism is not the same thing as striving to be our best. Perfectionism is not about healthy achievement and growth; it's a shield.

~ Brene Brown

Name _____

Date _____

Managing Intense Anxiety Workbook

Module IV – Take-Away Skills

We have included skills for most of the handouts in each Module, *Conditions and Behavior* (1), *Frequency and Duration* (2), and/or *Accomplishment* (3) statements for each activity may be used in educational and/or treatment planning, and also used to measure progress toward goals. These Take-Away skills promote real life outcomes and behavioral changes. Feel free to add additional skills for each activity.

Examples

1. **Conditions and Behavior** – a skill or healthy habit to replace a previous less effective behavior/habit.
   - Now, I … *(less effective or undesired behavior)*
     when I … *(when do I do this?)*.
     Instead I will … *(more effective or desired new behavior)* in ___ out of ___ opportunities.
2. **Frequency and Duration** – a skill or healthy habit not necessarily tied to a condition or previous behavior.
   - I will *(describe the behavior)* _____ times per _____.
3. **Accomplishment** – an outcome that is a one-time accomplishment.
   - I will *(describe the accomplishment)* by _____ *(date)*.

Take-Away Skills Examples

Criticizing Myself 92
Conditions and Behavior
- Now, I … *intensely criticize myself*
  when I … *make a social blunder.*
  Instead I will … *stop and "brush it off" 4 out of 4 opportunities.*

Criticizing Others 93
Conditions and Behavior
- Now, I … *nag at my partner*
  when … *he does not fold the laundry to my standard.*
  Instead I will … *thank him for his help, 4 out of 4 opportunities.*

Handling Criticism from Others 94
Conditions and Behavior
- Now, I … *avoid answering my mother's phone calls*
  when … *she said something I felt was offensive.*
  Instead I will … *answer her phone calls, 4 out of 4 opportunities.*

Take-Away Skills Examples *(Continued)*

Perfectionistic Thinking 95
Conditions and Behavior
- Now, I … *over-exaggerate the consequences*
  when I … *make a mistake at work.*
  Instead I will … *stop and determine if my thought is rational, 4 out of 4 opportunities.*
- Now, I … *label myself as a failure*
  when I … *receive feedback about a project.*
  Instead I will … *accept the feedback as a learning tool, 4 out of 4 opportunities.*

Perfectionism Affirmations 99
Accomplishment
- *I will make a collage honoring my positive qualities, by March 31st.*
Frequency and Duration
- I will … *tell myself a realistic affirmation 1 time every morning for 1 month.*

Perfectionistic Contract 100
Accomplishment
- *I will agree to do the best I can without needing to be perfect and sign the Perfectionistic Contract by the end of the month.*
Conditions and Behavior
- Now, I … *procrastinate*
  when I … *have to submit a paper.*
  Instead I will … *refer to my Perfectionistic Contract and let it go, 4 out of 4 opportunities.*

My Perfectionistic Moments 104
Conditions and Behavior
- Now, I … *do not not meet my deadlines*
  when I … *overthink my projects.*
  Instead I will … *begin sooner and turn my project in on time 4 out of 4 opportunities.*
- Now, I … *say "no" out of fear that I will not be "good" at it*
  when … *my partner asks me to try a new class with her.*
  Instead I will … *say "yes" and try it anyway, 4 out of 4 opportunities.*
Frequency and Duration
- I will … *try one new sport one time every month for three months.*
- I will … *record my Perfectionistic Moments in a log, 1 time every day for a week.*
- I will … *do one thing I have avoided doing because of my fear of being "bad" at it, one time a week for a month.*

Perfectionism Scale
Introduction and Directions

People often perceive of perfectionism as something positive and admirable. This is true to a certain point, but beyond that it can cause tremendous self-induced stress and anxiety. Perfectionism often creates an unhealthy need to set unrealistic standards, to work toward goals that are unachievable, to never make a mistake, and to be overly critical about self and others.

This scale contains 24 statements designed to help you explore if and how you tend to be perfectionistic. Read each item carefully and decide how much the statement describes you. In each of the choices listed, circle the number of your response.

In the following example, the circled number 2 indicates the statement is True for the person completing the scale.

	True	NOT True
1. I am extremely critical of myself	(2)	1

This is not a test and there are no right or wrong answers. Do not spend too much time thinking about your answers. Your initial response will be the most true for you. Be sure to respond to every statement.

(Turn to the next page and begin.)

Perfectionism Scale

	True	NOT True
1. I am extremely critical of myself	2	1
2. I hate myself if I don't get everything perfect	2	1
3. I take myself very seriously	2	1
4. I am very conscientious	2	1
5. I don't like to be criticized	2	1
6. I have an "all-or-nothing" approach	2	1

Scale C = _____

	True	NOT True
7. I delay projects because I'm concerned I can't do a perfect job	2	1
8. I tend to let myself down no matter how well I do	2	1
9. I expect the same standards I have for myself from those around me	2	1
10. I feel that everything in my life must be perfect	2	1
11. I believe that if I do anything in an average way would be shameful	2	1
12. My worth is tied to my accomplishments	2	1

Scale S = _____

	True	NOT True
13. I avoid answering questions because I may say something stupid	2	1
14. I believe mistakes are personal defects	2	1
15. I focus on my mistakes, not accomplishments	2	1
16. When looking at the past, I only think about my failures	2	1
17. I have a fear of not doing everything in a perfect way	2	1
18. I don't accept when others make mistakes	2	1

Scale M = _____

	True	NOT True
19. I become very upset when I do not reach my goals	2	1
20. I set unrealistic goals for myself	2	1
21. I set unrealistic goals for others	2	1
22. Anything less than meeting a goal perfectly is a failure	2	1
23. I drive myself to reach higher standards	2	1
24. I want to be the best in everything I do	2	1

Scale G = _____

Go to the Scoring Directions

Perfectionism Scale
Scoring Directions

Perfectionism creates a set of self-defeating thought patterns that push you to try to achieve unrealistically high goals.

The *Perfectionism Scale* is designed to help you figure out if you are a 'perfectionist' and explore some ways you tend to create your own anxiety. On the scale, add the numbers that you circled in each section and write the scores on each of the TOTAL lines. You will receive a total in the range from 6 to 12. Then, transfer those numbers to the space below. :

- **C Critical Total**   = _____
- **S Standards Total**   = _____
- **M Mistakes Total**   = _____
- **G Goals Total**   = _____

Profile Interpretation

Individual Total	Result	Indications
6 – 7	Low	If you scored in the LOW range, you do not show many perfectionistic traits.
8 – 10	Moderate	If you scored in the MODERATE range, you show some perfectionistic traits.
11 – 12	High	If you scored in the HIGH range, you show many perfectionistic traits.

Scale Descriptions

Critical – People scoring high on this scale are very critical about themselves and other people.

Standards – People scoring high on this scale set performance standards that are unrealistic and often unachievable.

Mistakes – People scoring high on this scale want to be flawless and never make a mistake.

Goals – People scoring high on this scale set unrealistic goals for themselves and for other people.

Criticizing Myself

At one time or another, all people find themselves in positions where they will be evaluated, and possibly criticized. People set very high standards for themselves and then they are critical when they are unable to achieve their goals. They never feel as if they are good enough or doing enough.

Complete the table to explore when you tend to be self-critical, if you are too self-critical, and an action plan to be less self-critical.

When do you tend to be critical of yourself?	Are you being too critical of yourself in this situation? Explain	What action plan can you have to be less critical of yourself?
Example: When I speak up at a meeting and then I don't like what I said or how I said it.	Maybe. Other people seemed to like what I had to say and agreed with me.	I have to remember that I believed in what I said and it's okay if some people didn't agree with me.

> *I'm always criticizing and only see the mistakes.*
> ~ **David Chang**

How does this quote apply to you? _____
_____
_____

To whom else in your life does this quote apply? _____
_____
_____

Perfectionism

Criticizing Others

At one time or another, all people find themselves in positions where they will be evaluating, and possibly criticizing other people. Perfectionists are very critical about others and are often harsh and judgmental in their criticisms of others.

Complete the table that follows to explore to whom you give criticism, how you handle it, and how you could handle it better.

With whom are you very critical?	Why are you critical of this person?	How can you perceive this person differently?
Example: My partner.	My partner doesn't load the dishwasher the way I like.	I can appreciate the effort and be glad I don't have to do it. It doesn't have to be loaded perfectly to clean the dishes.

> *Every human being is entitled to courtesy and consideration. Constructive criticism is not only to be expected but sought.*
> **~ Margaret Chase Smith**

What can you learn from this quotation? _____

_____

To whom else in your life does this quote apply? _____

_____

Managing Intense Anxiety Workbook

Handling Criticism from Others

Constructive criticism can be very important in becoming more self-aware and identifying ways you can improve yourself. Many people who are perfectionistic view constructive criticism very harshly, react defensively, and then become even more self-critical.

Complete the table that follows to explore from whom you receive criticism, how you handle it, and how you could handle it better.

From whom do you receive criticism?	How do you handle the criticism?	What are the ways you can handle the criticism better?
Example: My best friend disagrees and criticizes my political views.	I become angry and cancel all of our future plans until I'm not angry anymore.	I need to say "I respect your point of view and I hope you can respect mine. Let's not discuss it more!"

> *Criticism may not be agreeable, but it is necessary. It fulfils the same function as pain in the human body. It calls attention to an unhealthy state of things.*
> ~ **Winston Churchill**

What are your thoughts about the above quotation? _____

_____

_____

Perfectionistic Thinking

Perfectionistic thinking comes in many different forms. Some of the various forms are described below.

For each one, think about if and how you exhibit each type of thinking and provide examples from your daily life. Be honest with yourself!

Should Statements *(Example: I should never make a mistake.)* _____
_____
_____
_____
_____
_____

Catastrophic Thinking *(Example: If I make a mistake, people will laugh at me and I can't stand to be humiliated.)* _____
_____
_____
_____
_____
_____

Over-Exaggerating *(Example: If I don't do this perfectly, my boss will fire me.)* _____
_____
_____
_____
_____
_____

All-or-Nothing Thinking *(Example: Everything I do must be 100% perfect or it is no good. If I can't do it, it's because I am weak or a failure.)* _____
_____
_____
_____
_____
_____

> *ASK YOURSELF: How is it possible to always do something perfectly when it's something new or unfamiliar, or when it involves uncertainty?*

How I Feel When I am Being a Perfectionist

People say they can recognize when they are being perfectionistic.
Through self-awareness, you can do the same.

Below, identify your negative feelings associated with your perfectionism.

How I Feel	How Will I Know	How I Can Reverse It
Example: Sad / Depressed.	*I begin to feel tired and irritable.*	*I can reverse my negative thinking.*
Sad / Depressed		
Anxious		
Angry		
Frustrated		
Scared		
Other		

Which feeling do you experience most often when being perfectionistic?

___

People striving for excellence in a healthy way view mistakes as an opportunity to grow. They understand that mistakes are part of the learning process and they accept them.

Consequences of perfectionism are that it inhibits one, keeps one from taking risks, reduces the ability to innovate and create, and stops playfulness and the desire to dream.

To which of the items in the above two paragraphs can you relate?

___

___

Perfectionism

Perfectionistic Thoughts

It is important to document the perfectionistic thoughts that pop into your head. Some of these might include such thoughts as *People will laugh at me*. Or *I'm a bad person if I don't reach my goals!*

In the thought bubbles, write some of your perfectionistic thoughts.

What themes do you notice? _____
_____
_____

Managing Intense Anxiety Workbook

I Must Be Perfect

Many people feel that they must be perfect, or they will do everything in their power to try and be perfect. Think about the many ways in which you attempt to be perfect and how these ways limit you from what you aspire to achieve in your life and career.

Think about the ways you attempt to be perfect.

Ways I Seek Perfectionism	How I Try to Be Perfect	How These Ways Limit Me Personally & Professionally	How I Can Be Satisfied If I'm Not Perfect
Example: *Procrastination.*	*I keep thinking about assignments until I am late turning them in.*	*My supervisor has stopped giving me assignments to do.*	*I can begin sooner and not overthink the assignments.*
Procrastination			
Being too cautious			
Checking for mistakes			
Inability to take safe risks			
Worrying about small details			
Inability to try new things			
Other			

Perfectionism Affirmations

It can be helpful to create some realistic affirmations to remind you about perfectionism.

We've given you the first three. Create your own and/or brainstorm with others. Cut them out and put them on your refrigerator, tape them to your computer monitor, or stick them in your wallet, as reminders.

I don't have to be perfect!	I will do the best I can and hopefully finish on time!	The world has GREY Not just BLACK and WHITE

Managing Intense Anxiety Workbook

A Perfectionistic Contract

By filling in the blanks on this contract, you will agree to live the rest of your life doing the best you can, and not always needing to be perfect.

Complete the following contract and sign and date it. Keep it handy so that you can see it daily.

A Perfectionist Contract

I, _____, agree not to be perfectionist at home, with friends, or anywhere.
    NAME

I will try not to be perfectionistic by doing any of the following:

- I will not set standards that are too high. I will do this by:

  _____

  _____

- I will not be too critical of myself and others. I will do this by:

  _____

  _____

- I will not be angry or disappointed in myself when I make mistakes. I will do this by:

  _____

  _____

- I will not set goals that are too lofty to achieve. I will do this by:

  _____

  _____

_____   _____
               NAME   DATE

Perfectionism

The Good and the Bad

People who exhibit perfectionistic tendencies have a difficult time realizing how these tendencies are harming them. They say things like *"I like to do things well"* and *"It makes me feel good."*

Below, based on your perfectionism, identify the ways it IS helpful to you, and the ways it IS NOT helpful to you.

My perfectionism is helpful to me ...

My perfectionism is NOT helpful to me ...

Which list is larger? Why? _____

_____

_____

Underlying Perfectionistic Reasons

Sometimes people who are perfectionistic have deep underlying reasons for thinking they must be perfect.

These questions will guide you through the process of uncovering these reasons. Think about why you are perfectionistic.

If I make a mistake, I think …

If I make a mistake, people will think …

If I don't reach very high standards, I will …

If I don't reach high standards, people will think …

If I don't reach my goals, I will …

If I don't reach my goals, people will think …

If I am criticized by others, I will …

> *Striving for excellence motivates you; striving for perfection is demoralizing!*
> **~ Harriet Braiker**

What is your opinion about the above quotation? _____

_____

_____

Perfectionism

Small Steps in Setting Realistic Goals

If you are a perfectionist, you might set goals that are much too lofty for you or anyone to achieve. It is important that you take small steps in setting goals that are achievable, then set new goals. You will only get frustrated if you set unrealistic goals and are unable to achieve them. Breaking goals into small manageable steps helps.

In the steps that follow, set a long-term achievable goal and several short-term goals for one aspect of your life.

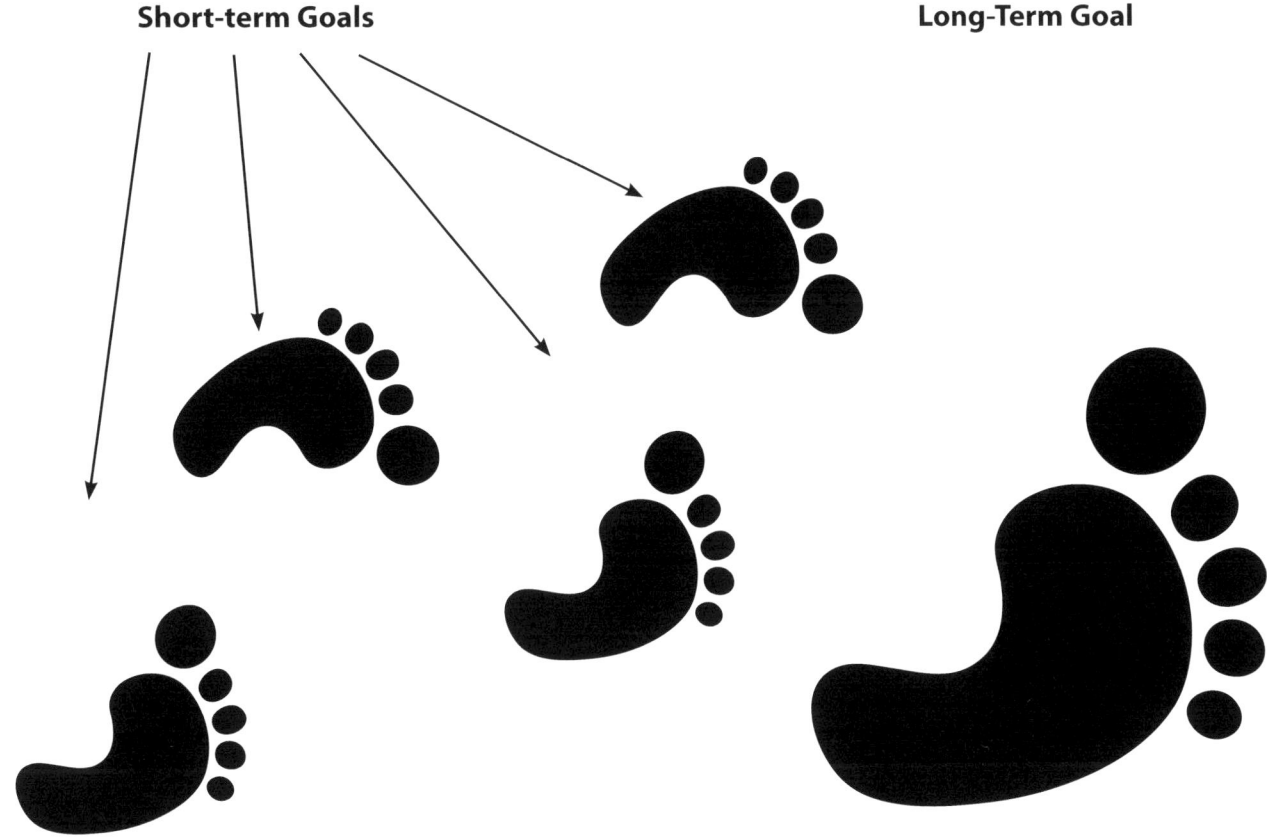

> *When it is obvious that the goals cannot be reached, don't adjust the goals, adjust the action steps.*
> ~ **Confucius**

How would the above quotation assist people who are perfectionists?

_____

_____

_____

My Perfectionistic Moments

Most people feel perfectionistic about some minor things, but people who function well understand the situations in which they are way too perfectionistic and how this affects their daily functioning and relationships.

What are some of the situations in which you feel like you are way too perfectionistic?

My Perfectionistic Moment Situation	Why I Feel or Act This Way	How It Affects Me & People Around Me	How I Could Be Less Perfectionistic
Example: I will not turn in work projects until I check the details at least five times.	I worry that my work will have mistakes and then I will feel embarrassed.	I don't get my work done and my boss gets frustrated with me.	I could check my work once or twice, and trust that it is okay.

Which moments are negatively affecting your life the most? _____

_____

_____

_____

Perfectionism

Respecting and Loving Myself

To overcome perfectionism, it is important to be aware of how you love and respect yourself. In the spaces that follow, identify the ways you respect and love yourself.

In each of the blocks that follow, write words that describe your most positive qualities.
(Example: artistic, smart, compassionate, caring, love for children, etc.)

My People Skills

My Work / Volunteer Skills

My Personality Characteristics

My Special Gifts

The Positive Me

People who are perfectionistic thinkers tend to focus on their negative qualities and mistakes. However, they probably have many more positive qualities and successes than negative qualities and failures.

Identify a negative quality, why you don't like it, and then list four positive qualities related to the negative one.

Settings	Things I Don't Like About Me Related to This Setting and Why	What I Do Like About Me Related to This Setting
My Job or Volunteer Work	1.	1. 2. 3. 4.
My Home Life	1.	1. 2. 3. 4.
My Relationships	1.	1. 2. 3. 4.

Which aspects in the last column, do you like most about yourself and why? _____

_____

_____

_____

Save this page and post it somewhere in sight to remind yourself of your positive qualities.

MODULE V

Erasing the Stigma of Mental Health Issues

Stigma's power lies in silence. The silence that persists when discussion and action should be taking place …

~ *M. B. Dallocchio*

Name _____

Date _____

Erasing the Stigma of Mental Health Issues
Introduction

A stigma is extreme social disapproval of some type of personal characteristic or a belief that is not considered socially "acceptable." People who have a particular attribute considered unwanted by society are rejected or stigmatized as a result of the attribute. People who experience intense anxiety and panic attacks in the past are often judged unfairly to be "crazy," nervous, unrealistically worried, afraid around other people, phobic, and/or unstable. These judgments, or social stigmas, can cause people who experience these issues to feel devalued as human beings. They are often ostracized from activities, rejected in social situations, stereotyped, minimized in the workplace, and shunned by others. People experiencing the stigma of intense anxiety issues often feel extreme physical and psychological distress.

People who stigmatize and/or stereotype others bring about unfair treatment. This unfair treatment can be very obvious. For example, people make negative comments or laugh. On the other hand, this unfair treatment can be very subtle. For example, people assume that someone who experiences anxiety issues is fearful and nervous all the time, and they avoid or shun that person.

Stigmas affect a large percentage of people throughout the world. Some of the more common stigmas are associated with physical disabilities, mental health issues, age, body type, gender, sexual orientation, nationality, religion, family, ethnicity, race, religion, financial status, social subcultures, and conduct. Stigmas set people apart from society and produce feelings in them of shame and isolation. People who are stigmatized are often considered socially unacceptable and they suffer prejudice, rejection, avoidance, and discrimination.

WHAT CAN BE DONE?

Fear of judgment and ridicule about anxiety issues often compels individuals and their families to hide from society rather than face criticism, shunning, labeling, and stereotyping. Instead of seeking treatment, they struggle in silence. Let's discuss some ways you can combat the stereotypes and stigmas that are associated with these issues.

- You and your loved ones have choices. You can decide who is to know about your anxiety and what to tell them. You need not feel guilty, ashamed, or embarrassed.
- You are not alone. Remember that many other people are coping with a similar situation.
- Look into or start a support group to meet others who experience what you do.
- Seek help and remember that the activities in this workbook and treatment from medical professionals can help you to have a productive education and career, and to live a satisfying life.
- Be proactive and surround yourself with supportive people – people you can trust. Social isolation is a negative side effect of the stigma linked to moodiness. Isolating yourself and discontinuing enjoyable activities will not help.

HOW CAN THIS SECTION HELP ME?

Managing Intense Anxiety Workbook is designed to help you deal more effectively with your issues, and this module is specifically designed to help you overcome the stigma attached to those issues. Complete the activities that follow to feel better about yourself, feel content, and become more resilient in the face of stress in your life.

Two Types of Mental Health Stigma

Mental health stigma can be divided into two types:

1. *Social stigma* is characterized by prejudicial attitudes and discriminating behavior directed towards individuals with mental health issues.

2. *Perceived stigma* is the internalizing by the people with mental health issues of their understanding of discrimination.

What do you think are the differences between these two types of stigmas?

___

___

___

___

Describe a time when you faced prejudice or discrimination because you experienced anxiety.

___

___

___

___

Describe a time when you felt like you were at a disadvantage because you experienced anxiety

___

___

___

___

Often one perceives others' stigmatizing, or exaggerates others' or their own reactions.

Managing Intense Anxiety Workbook

The Stigma of Intense Anxiety — THE PAST

People who experience anxiety in their lives are prone to reoccurring symptoms. When this happens, they often have a stigma placed on them by other people. Often the stigma attached to this issue stops one from moving forward - being unable to talk about it for fear of being judged or labeled. We can erase the stigma of any mental health issue by starting to discuss it with one person at a time, and taking the time to explain the anxiety you lived through in the past.

Let's start with people with whom you have already shared your story.

With whom have you discussed your issues?	What did you say?	What was this person's reaction? What did the person say?	How did you feel?
Family			
Friends			
Acquaintances			
People in your community or your house of worship			
Other			
Other			

If any one of the above reacted in a negative way, to what do you attribute that reaction?

_____

_____

_____

Erasing the Stigma of Mental Health Issues

The Stigma of Intense Anxiety — THE PRESENT

If you are yet to tell your story to people, now may be the time. This workbook has helped you to organize your thoughts and feelings about your anxiety. One of the ways to erase this stigma is to talk about it and let others know that people who have intense anxiety are just like anyone else who have some type of an issue.

Perhaps it is time to talk with other people whom you trust and/or feel safe.

Person with whom you might discuss your issue?	What would you say to this person?	What do you think this person's reaction might be?	What could you gain or lose by discussing it with this person?
Family			
Friends			
Acquaintances			
People in your community or your house of worship			
Other			
Other			

Brainstorm this with the group:

At what point, in a serious relationship, is it time to discuss your issues?

Managing Intense Anxiety Workbook

Speak Your Mind

> *Follow the path of the unsafe, independent thinker.*
> *Expose your ideas to the danger of controversy.*
> *Speak your mind and fear less the label of 'crackpot' than the stigma of conformity.*
> **~ Thomas J. Watson**

What does the above quotation mean to you? _____
_____
_____
_____
_____

Do you ever speak your mind? Why or Why Not? _____
_____
_____
_____
_____

Are you worried about being labeled? Explain. _____
_____
_____
_____
_____

How can you expose your ideas to others? _____
_____
_____
_____
_____

What is keeping you from telling your story? _____
_____
_____
_____
_____

If We Stamp Out the Stigma ...

If we stamp out the stigma attached to mental health issues, shed the shame and eliminate the fear, then we open the door for people to speak freely about what they are feeling and thinking.

~ Jaletta Albright Desmond

**Journal your thoughts about the quotation above,
and how you can do your part to erase the stigma of anxiety issues.**

_____
_____
_____
_____
_____
_____
_____
_____
_____
_____
_____
_____
_____
_____
_____
_____
_____
_____
_____
_____
_____
_____
_____
_____

Managing Intense Anxiety Workbook

Glenn Close said …

"The most powerful way to change someone's view is to meet them … People who do come out and talk about mental illness, that's when healing can really begin. You can lead a productive life."

Name a time when you have changed someone else's view – about anything. _____
_____
_____

How did that feel to you? _____
_____
_____

Name a time you were tempted to talk about your anxiety issues, but didn't? Why not? _____
_____
_____

Write about a situation in which you talked about your anxiety issues? _____
_____
_____
_____
_____

How did that feel? _____
How did it work out? _____
_____

Who is a trusted person you can talk with and begin to heal? _____
Anyone else?_____
Who is a trusted person you can ask for a referral of someone to talk with in order to begin to heal?_____
_____

Anyone else?_____

In an ideal world, how can you lead a more stable life?_____
_____
_____

How can you contribute to changing stigma?_____
_____
_____

Erasing the Stigma of Mental Health Issues

Effects of Anxiety Issues

Check out these harmful effects of the stigma of intense anxiety.
Write on the lines next to each item if it has affected you in some way and how.

1. Lack of understanding by family _____
   _____

2. Lack of understanding by friends _____
   _____

3. Lack of understanding by co-workers, supervisors and/or customers _____
   _____

4. Discrimination at work _____
   _____

5. Inability to join community programs _____
   _____

6. Inability to manage the anxiety _____
   _____

7. Pressure from friends _____
   _____

8. The belief that you will never be able to succeed or that you can't improve your situation.
   _____
   _____

On the line of the corresponding number, write the name of a person you can speak to, a person who might help to support you about each of the situations you noted above. Add a reason you've chosen that person.

1. _____
2. _____
3. _____
4. _____
5. _____
6. _____
7. _____
8. _____

Managing Intense Anxiety Workbook

The Stigma of Going to a Mental Health Therapist

Many people have pre-conceived ideas about anyone seeking therapy.

Do you know of anyone who has gone to a mental health therapist? Write what you know about the experience. _____
_____
_____

Here are some facts about mental health and mental health therapy.

- Mental health includes how you act, feel, and think in different situations.
- Mental health problems can be caused by many different things including medical health issues, abuse (emotional, physical, verbal, sexual), stress, worry, loss of a relationship, food issues, ADHD, STD's, family changes, addictions, traumatic event, problems, wanting to build up self-confidence, etc.
- If someone goes to a mental health therapist, this does NOT mean the person is crazy. Mental health therapists treat people the same as any other medical doctor treats problems.
- There needs to be a good connection between you and the therapist. Your therapist should be someone you feel you can trust.
- This might take a few meetings and/or a few therapists, to find the right one for you.
- Non-judgmental people who truly care about you will not judge you in a negative way. They will be proud of you for seeking help.
- The therapist does not assume that you have a mental illness. The therapist assumes something is troubling you, knows that no one leads a perfect life, and admires you for trying to make changes in your life.
- The therapist's job is to help you understand what's going on.
- The therapist will not tell you how to live your life, or how to think, act, or believe.
- The therapist is not an advice-giver, but will help you think about how to increase your quality of life.
- The therapist may have some thoughts, and with you, will help you make changes.
- The therapist can help you to increase your life management skills.
- The therapist will help you recognize and express your feelings in a healthy way.
- The only person who can "fix" your problems is you, but a therapist will help you with an action plan.
- The mental health therapist may suggest that you see a medical doctor for medication.
- Therapy can be a slow or long process. Being open and honest, and wanting to feel better, will make the difference.

Place an X by the facts that you were not aware of.

What are your concerns about talking with a mental health therapist? _____
_____
_____

After learning about these facts, can you make a commitment to speak with a counselor or therapist?

*signature*_____

Will You Speak Out?

> *Ten people who speak make more noise than ten thousand who are silent.*
> ~ Napoleon Bonaparte

How can YOU speak out to erase the stigma about people who have intense anxiety?

_____
_____
_____
_____
_____
_____
_____
_____
_____
_____

Brainstorm with a few other people about how you can speak out to erase the stigma of intense anxiety?

_____
_____
_____
_____
_____
_____
_____
_____
_____
_____

My Negative Thoughts

You can begin to overcome the stigma related to anxiety issues by refusing to worry about what others think. When you are worried about what others say about you, or might say about you, you will have a difficult time enjoying life.

Explore and write about the negative thoughts that go through your head about others and what they think of you?

Others think I am …

Others don't think I can …

Others possibly find me …

I think others might be afraid or wary of me because …

Others label me as …

This makes me feel …

Now that you have written these thoughts, take a big heavy black marker and put a big **X** through all of the thoughts above. When these negative thoughts come into your head, picture that big X, reminding you not to worry about what others think.

Focus on Your Strengths

You can do many things to help fight the stigma associated with your anxiety issues. You can focus on your strengths rather than your limitations. Demonstrate to others, and yourself, that you have a great deal to offer.

In the spaces that follow, identify some of your strengths. You have much to share, so take a few minutes to think about and write about some of your greatest strengths.

My strengths related to the community:

_____

_____

My strengths related to relationships with others:

_____

_____

My strengths related to my work or volunteer job:

_____

_____

My strengths related to creativity:

_____

_____

My strengths related to special skills I possess:

_____

_____

How can you share these strengths to show others that even though you may have anxiety issues, you are a capable, talented human being?

_____

_____

Managing Intense Anxiety Workbook

Ways I Try to Minimize My Anxiety Issues

Many people dealing with the stress that occurs from intense anxiety will try a variety of ways to minimize its stigma.

Complete the following table to explore the various ways in which you minimize your issues and how this makes you feel. Describe some better ways to cope.

Ways I Minimize the Stigma of Intense Anxiety	The Effect This Has on Others and Myself	A Better Way to Cope
Example: I pretend that nothing is wrong with me.	Others think I should just 'get over' my anxiety and move on. It's not that easy and it upsets me when they say that.	Explain that I've been having some anxiety issues and I'm working on learning how to manage them.
I pretend that nothing is wrong with me.		
I don't ask for help.		
Angry I say things like "Nothing can ever help me."		
I do not talk about my anxiety issues.		
I laugh and make jokes about my anxiety.		
I often avoid people.		
Other		
Other		

Ways I Am Treated

Think about some of the ways that people treat you because of the symptoms you show due to your anxieties. In the spaces below, explore the various ways people treat you.

Write about those who treat you unfairly and why.

I am criticized by my family and/or friends …

[ ]

I am ignored by my family and/or friends …

[ ]

I encounter problems at work …

[ ]

I encounter problems at home …

[ ]

I am subjected to teasing or harassment …

[ ]

I am laughed at …

[ ]

I treat myself unfairly by …

[ ]

I treat myself fairly by …

[ ]

Managing Intense Anxiety Workbook

Self-Doubt

Don't let stigma of anxiety issues create self-doubt and shame. One of the most important ways to minimize this stigma is to explore how you doubt yourself. Self-doubt almost always stems from a lack of understanding or from past experiences, rather than information based on the facts. Feeling ashamed, embarrassed, or guilty because of what you experienced can be self-defeating.

How does the stress associated with living with intense anxiety issues cause you to doubt yourself and how can you control your self-doubt in a positive and strong way?

Ways I Doubt Myself	How This Negatively Affects Me	What I Can Do About it
Example: I am very anxious when I need to speak up in public, even if it's only with a few people.	I avoid it, and this is holding me back from advancing at work.	I can search online for a local class to take a speaking course.

> *However you arrive at the ability to ignore self-doubt - if you can acquire it or possess it or find it or discover it – move beyond self-doubt.*
>
> **~ Dwight Yoakum**

How do you relate to this quotation? _____

_____

_____

A Poster about the STIGMA of People Who Experience Anxiety

In the space that follows, draw a collage of pictures, symbols, and/or words, of how you believe you are being stigmatized by others.

A Poster about ACCEPTANCE of People who Experience Anxiety

In the space that follows, draw a collage of pictures, symbols, and/or words, of what you believe that the stress related to anxiety looks like when you are accepted.

DE-STIGMA-TIZE with the Facts about Mental Health Issues

Myth: Mental health issues are rare.
   Fact: Mental health issues are not rare and affect nearly everyone either directly or indirectly.

Myth: People with mental health issues are unable to lead successful, productive lives.
   Fact: Most people with mental health issues respond to treatment, learn to cope with and manage their problems, and go on to lead productive and fulfilling lives.

Myth: People who have mental health issues will not get better.
   Fact: Once diagnosed, mental health issues are treatable. While they are not always cured, they can be managed effectively. Most people with mental health issues live productive and positive lives. Many receive therapy and medications. Individuals with severe or persistent mental health issues who do not respond well to therapy or meds may require more support, or different therapists or meds, and they do well; and some may not function as highly as others.

Myth: People with mental health problems are violent and unpredictable.
   Fact: While some people who suffer from mental health issues do commit antisocial acts, a mental health issue does not equal criminality or violence - despite the media's tendency to emphasize a suspected link. People with mental illness are no more likely to commit violence than anyone in the general public, but they are more likely to be victimized and are more likely to inflict violent actions on themselves.

Myth: Mental health issues happen because of bad parenting or personal weakness.
   Fact: The main risk factors for mental health issues are not bad parenting or personal weakness but rather genetics, severe and prolonged stress (such as physical or sexual abuse), or other environmental influences (such as birth trauma or head injury).

Myth: Treatments for mental health issues is not usually effective.
   Fact: The effectiveness of any treatment depends on a number of factors including the type of mental issue and the particular needs of the individual. A combination of psychiatric medication and psychotherapy, or social interventions are the most effective way to treat mental health issues.

Myth: Mental health issues are caused by everyday stressors.
   Fact: It may seem that stress is responsible for mental health issues; however, there is no one clear cause of mental health issues. Rather, it is a result of complex interactions between psychological, biological, genetic and social factors. Stress, stigma, and lack of support can make it worse for the individual.

Myth: Mental health issues are always hereditary.
   Fact: Some mental health issues include a genetic component, which results in a predisposition or vulnerability toward the illness among children and siblings, but environment also plays a key role in the development of certain mental health issues. If someone in one's family has mental health issues, that person will be at higher risk.

If you start to experience the symptoms of a mental health issue, it is important for you to see a medical professional to determine if you have a problem that will require treatment. If you know of anyone who seems to have symptoms of a mental health issue, urge that person to do the same.

Coping with the Stigma of an Intense Anxiety Issue

Get treatment. Don't let the fear of being *labeled* with an anxiety issue prevent you from seeking help. Treatment can provide relief by identifying and reducing symptoms that interfere with your work and personal life. How can you get treatment? _____
_____
_____
_____

Don't let stigma create self-doubt and shame. If you are buying into the stigma, you will have the mistaken belief that your issue is a sign of personal weakness, or that *you should* be able to control it better. How can you have less self-doubt? _____
_____
_____
_____

How can you have less shame? _____
_____
_____
_____

Don't isolate yourself. Have the courage to confide in your family members, friends, partner, clergy, therapist, or other members of your community. Who can you reach out to and who can you trust for the compassion, support, and understanding you need? _____
_____
_____
_____

Get help at work. If you are having intense anxiety and it is affecting your work, confidentially talk with a supervisor, explain what you are doing to help yourself, and find out what plans and programs that are available might help. _____
_____
_____
_____

If you and others are willing, share responses.

Speak Out Against Stigmas

Your openness can help instill courage in others who are facing anxiety issues, and it will help to educate the public about the effect that these issues have on you personally. Speaking out for, and about yourself, advocates for others who might have these issues and it can be beneficial to you at the same time.

Think about some of the ways you might let your voice be heard about stigmas and their damaging effects on people. For each of the items, list the ways that you could speak out against stigmas.

Express your opinions at events. What events are planned in your place of employment where you might speak out against stigmas? _____
_____
_____

At what events in your community might you volunteer to speak out against stigmas? _____
_____
_____

You could write an informative feature article or letter to the editor of a local newspaper or magazine. What would you say? _____
_____
_____

You could blog about stigmas on the Internet. How can you do this? _____
_____
_____

What are some other ways to speak out against stigmas? _____
_____
_____

How do you think this will benefit others? _____
_____
_____

How will it benefit you? _____
_____
_____

Whole Person Associates is the leading publisher of training resources for professionals who empower people to create and maintain healthy lifestyles. Our creative resources will help you work effectively with your clients in the areas of stress management, wellness promotion, mental health, and life skills.

Please visit us at our web site: **WholePerson.com**. You can check out our entire line of products, place an order, request our print catalog, and sign up for our monthly special notifications.

Whole Person Associates
800-247-6789
Books@WholePerson.com